D1346303

DES MACHALE is associate Professor of Mathematics at University College Cork and the author of over thirty humour books. He is famous for his defence of the joke against the politically correct, and is a regular delegate at humour conferences the world over.

Wit is a personal labour of love – a collection of quotations culled over a period of twenty years.

To Barry
        Happy Birthday 2007
            Best wishes
                from Lyndon & Kate.

Reviews of Des MacHale's *Wit*

"Full of delight."
Horace Bent, *The Bookseller*

"A good and comprehensive anthology
of bons mots."
Peter Mckay, *The Mail on Sunday* humour books of the year

"A contender for Book of the Month."
Matthew Norman, *The Guardian*

"Wit...unlike most other books of humorous
quotations, is actually funny."
Paul Vallely, *The Independent*

"It's good to learn that Churchill thought
De Gaulle resembled a female llama suprised in
her bath."
Ian McIntyre, *The Times*

Wit

Humorous quotation books from Prion

Des MacHale
Wit
Wit Hits The Spot
(previously entitled More Wit)
Wit on Target
(previously entitled Yet More Wit)
Wit — The Last Laugh
Wit Rides Again
Ultimate Wit

Aubrey Dillon Malone
The Cynic's Dictionary

MichaelPowell
High Society
Funny Money

Michelle Lovric
Women's Wicked Wit

Gert de Ley & David Potter
Don't Do It!
Do Unto Others...then run

Wit

Des MacHale

PRION

This book is dedicated to my brother Bennie with affection.

First published in Great Britain in 1996
First published in paperback in 1997 and reprinted 10 times
This edition published 2006 by

Prion
an imprint of the
Carlton Publishing Group
20 Mortimer Street
London W1T 3JW

2 4 6 8 10 9 7 5 3 1

Compilation copyright © Des MacHale 1994, 1996
Design copyright © Carlton Publishing Group

ISBN-13: 978-1-85375-589-7
ISBN-10: 1-85375-589-3

A catalogue record for this book is available from the British Library.

Printed in Great Britain by Mackays

Contents

Introduction

Over the last twenty years or so, I have been collecting humorous quotations from books, magazines, newspapers, radio, television, films, records, word of mouth, and any other source that one can possibly imagine. This book is the result of my labours and it has given me a lot of fun.

A good humorous quotation in my opinion should have several qualities.

i   First of all it should be funny – it should provoke laughter or at least a smile. Too many books of humorous quotations are shamelessly padded with substandard material that is not even remotely funny. I humbly submit that this book is different.

ii   It should be short and pithy, for brevity is the soul of wit: the average quotation in this book has about fourteen words, but I have not resisted the temptation to include just a few longer quotes of exceptional merit.

iii   It should be free-standing i.e. it must be independent of the context in which it arises. This rather stringent requirement will undoubtedly eliminate some old favourites of yours and mine, but look at it this way – if the explanation of why a quotation is funny because of where it arises is actually longer than the quotation itself, is it really worth the bother?

For the convenience of speakers, writers and others who require humorous quotations to spice up their material, this book has been divided into twenty wide-ranging chapters and there is also an index listing all the quotations attributed to each individual. This naturally begs the question – who was the greatest wit of all time? I have thought long and hard on this question and I have found it virtually impossible to choose a single name – doubtless very few people would agree on a single choice. Putting my neck on the chopping block, the most I will risk is the following opinion.

Oscar Wilde was the greatest wit of the nineteenth century and Woody Allen is the greatest wit of the twentieth century. Wilde's wit was sophisticated and clever, while Allen's wit is hilarious and down to earth, but I find it impossible to separate them in terms of merit. Perhaps it is fitting that the prize be shared between the Irish and the Jews – the two wittiest races that have ever lived. Interestingly, both Wilde and Allen ran into difficulties of a very unfunny nature towards the end of their careers. Perhaps this is the price to be paid for being a truly great wit.

In the second flight I would place Mark Twain, Evelyn Waugh, Ambrose Bierce, George Ade, Steven Wright,

Emo Philips, H.L. Mencken, Brendan Behan, Thomas Beecham, George Burns, Quentin Crisp, Noel Coward, Phyllis Diller, W.C. Fields, Dick Gregory, Spike Milligan, Groucho Marx, Joan Rivers, George Bernard Shaw, and Alexander Woollcott.

Honourable mention goes to the following: Robert Benchley, Max Beerbohm, Winston Churchill, Samuel Goldwyn, Bob Hope, Heinrich Heine, Samuel Johnson, Stephen Leacock, Ring Lardner, P.J. O'Rourke, Dorothy Parker, Rita Rudner, Sydney Smith, James Thurber and Lee Trevino.

I have not burdened the text with potted biographies of the contributors – not even birth dates or death dates, because such information is largely irrelevant to the humour, and in any case can easily be looked up elsewhere if needed. I honestly believe that this collection of well over two thousand humorous quotations that you, lucky reader, are about to immerse yourself in, is the best such collection ever assembled. I believe this so strongly that if you can provide me with a better and funnier collection, I will eat it, without seasoning. Enjoy!

Des MacHale
Cork

Art

Art

Abstract art is a product of the untalented, sold by the unprincipled, to the utterly bewildered.

Al Capp

I inherited a painting and a violin which turned out to be a Rembrandt and a Stradivarius. Unfortunately Rembrandt made lousy violins and Stradivarius was a terrible painter.

Tommy Cooper

Anyone who sees and paints a sky green and fields blue ought to be sterilised.

Adolf Hitler

Which painting in the National Gallery would I save if there was a fire? The one nearest the door of course.

George Bernard Shaw

The only thoroughly original ideas I have ever heard Mr Whistler express have had reference to his own superiority as a painter over painters greater than himself.

Oscar Wilde

She looks like the Venus de Milo; she is very old, has no teeth, and has white spots on her yellow skin.

Heinrich Heine

She is one of those ladies who pursue culture in bands, as though it were dangerous to meet it alone.

Edith Wharton

There is only one difference between a madman and me. I am not mad.

Salvador Dali

Art

He was as ugly as a gargoyle hewn by a drunken stonemason for the adornment of a Methodist Chapel in one of the vilest suburbs of Leeds or Wigan.

Max Beerbohm

You ask me, Sir, for a suitable institution to which you propose to leave your paintings. May I suggest an asylum for the blind?

James McNeill Whistler

I don't understand anything about the ballet. All I know is that during the intervals the ballerinas stink like horses.

Anton Chekhov

Post-Impressionist drawing is on the level of an untaught child of seven or eight years old, the sense of colour of a tea-tray painter, the method of a schoolboy who wipes his fingers on a slate after spitting on them.

Wilfred Blunt

I am lonesome. They are all dying. I have hardly a warm personal enemy left.

James McNeill Whistler

If it sells, it's art.

Frank Lloyd

Many excellent cooks are spoilt by going into the arts.

Paul Gauguin

All the arts in America are a gigantic racket run by unscrupulous men for unhealthy women.

Thomas Beecham

Can it be mere coincidence that so many of the best Post-Impressionists are Poles?

Patrick Murray

Art

There is nothing on earth more terrible than English music,
except English painting.

Heinrich Heine

There is only one difference between a madman and me.
The madman thinks he is sane. I know I am mad.

Salvador Dali

'Burn the museums!' This old revolutionary slogan can now
be realised by the museums themselves. A museum set on fire
would today attract the usual crowd that visits its exhibitions.
It calls not for the end of art but for the expansion of art
institutions to include the medium of combustion.

Harold Rosenberg

This is either a forgery or a damn clever original.

Frank Sullivan

Gerald Kelly made a last desperate attempt to persuade the
world he was an artist by marrying a model. But this device
deceived nobody.

Aleister Crowley

The goitrous, torpid and squinting husks provided by
Matisse in his sculpture are worthless except as tactful
decorations for a mental home.

Percy Wyndham-Lewis

Mr Whistler, with all his faults, was never guilty of writing a
line of poetry.

Oscar Wilde

Dada's art is just turpentine intoxication.

Marcel Duchamp

Art

The preponderance of women and homosexuals in the arts today signifies only the scurrying of rats near a dying body.

Shulamith Firestone

Salvador Dali seduced many ladies, particularly American ladies; but these seductions usually consisted of stripping them naked in his apartment, frying a couple of eggs, putting them on the woman's shoulders, and without a word showing them the door.

Luis Buñuel

Jeff Koon's work is the last bit of methane left in the intestine of the dead cow that is post-modernism.

Robert Hughes

Business and Money

I've been rich and I've been poor – rich is better.

Sophie Tucker

If you would like to know the value of money, go and try to borrow some.

Benjamin Franklin

I've got all the money I'll ever need if I die by four o'clock this afternoon.

Henny Youngman

October. This is one of the peculiarly dangerous months to speculate in stocks. Other dangerous months are July, January, September, April, November, May, March, June, December, August and February.

Mark Twain

When I was young I used to think that money was the most important thing in life. Now that I am old, I know it is.

Oscar Wilde

I owe much; I have nothing; the rest I leave to the poor.

François Rabelais

A lot of people become pessimists from financing optimists.

C. T. Jones

Money is just the poor man's credit card.

Marshall McLuhan

A man who has a million dollars is as well off as if he were rich.

Cleveland Amory

Business and Money

Dear *Reader's Digest*, we hardly know each other, yet I have been selected from so many millions to enter your free contest in which I may win £25,000. You have made me very happy.

Miles Kington

My luck is so bad that if I bought a cemetery, people would stop dying.

Ed Furgol

Undermine the entire economic structure of society by leaving the pay toilet door ajar so the next person can get in free.

Taylor Meade

I always arrive late at the office, but I make up for it by leaving early.

Charles Lamb

A verbal contract isn't worth the paper it's written on.
Samuel Goldwyn

It is only by not paying one's bills that one can hope to live in the memory of the commercial classes.

Oscar Wilde

Money can't buy you happiness, but it does bring you a more pleasant form of misery.

Spike Milligan

The light at the end of the tunnel is just the light of an oncoming train.

Robert Lowell

When I asked my accountant if anything could get me out of the mess I am in now, he thought for a long time. 'Yes,' he said, 'death would help'.

Robert Morley

They usually have two tellers in my local bank. Except when it's very busy, when they have one.

Rita Rudner

It is morally wrong to allow a sucker to keep his money.

W.C. Fields

Having a little inflation is like being a little bit pregnant.

Leon Henderson

Office Hours: 2 to 2.15 every other Wednesday.

George S. Kaufman

I rob banks because that's where the money is.

Willie Sutton

Statistics indicate that as a result of overwork, modern executives are dropping like flies on the nation's golf courses.

Ira Wallach

We were allowed to accept gifts of flowers, candies, jewels, furs, yachts, castles – but never money.

Quentin Crisp

I always travel first-class on the train. It's the only way to avoid one's creditors.

Seymour Hicks

If only God would give me a clear sign! Like making a large deposit in my name at a Swiss bank.

Woody Allen

I haven't reported my missing credit card to the police because whoever stole it is spending less than my wife.

Ilie Nastase

The holy passion of friendship is of so sweet and steady and loyal and enduring a nature that it will last through a whole lifetime, if not asked to lend money.

Mark Twain

You should always live within your income, even if you have to borrow to do so.

Josh Billings

All students of economics should learn about Marxism, just as all medical students should learn about venereal diseases.

C.K. Grant

Money is better than poverty, if only for financial reasons.

Woody Allen

One of the strangest things about life is that the poor, who need money the most, are the very ones that never have it.

Finley Peter Dunne

I wish that dear Karl could have spent some time acquiring capital instead of merely writing about it.

Jenny Marx

Blessed are the young, for they shall inherit the national debt.

Herbert Hoover

The first rule of business is – do other men for they would do you.

Charles Dickens

Any organisation is like a septic tank. The really big chunks always rise to the top.

John Imhoff

Business and Money

Never answer a letter until you get a second one on the same subject from the same person.

Michael O'Hagan

Tell your boss what you really think about him and the truth shall set you free.

Patrick Murray

I could have done the job myself in twenty minutes, but as things turned out I had to spend two days to find out why it had taken someone else three weeks to do it wrong.

J.L. McCafferty

If Bret Harte ever repaid a loan, the incident failed to pass into history.

Mark Twain

To make a long story short, there's nothing like having the boss walk in.

Doris Lilly

His insomnia was so bad, he couldn't sleep even during office hours.

Arthur Baer

What's the use of happiness? It can't buy you money.

Henny Youngman

Nothing is as irritating as the fellow who chats pleasantly to you while he's overcharging you.

Kin Hubbard

There are three easy ways of losing money – racing is the quickest, women the most pleasant, and farming the most certain.

Lord Amherst

Any man who has $10,000 left when he dies is a failure.

Errol Flynn

I don't owe a penny to a single soul – not counting tradesmen of course.

P.G. Wodehouse

I have enough money to last me the rest of my life – unless I have to buy something.

Jackie Mason

There are worse things in life than death. Have you ever spent an evening with an insurance salesman?

Woody Allen

God has mercifully withheld from humanity a foreknowledge of what will sell.

Bernard Miles

I'm living so far beyond my income that we may almost be said to be living apart.

e.e. cummings

The government incomes policy is as significant as a blush on a dead man's cheek.

Clive Jenkins

Today's payslip has more deductions than a Sherlock Holmes story.

Raymond J. Cvikota

Don't tell my mother I work in an advertising agency. She thinks I play the piano in a whorehouse.

Jacques Seguela

Business is often about killing your favourite children to allow the others to succeed.

John Harvey-Jones

There was a time when a fool and his money were soon parted, but now it happens to everybody.

Adlai Stevenson

If there is anyone to whom I owe money, I am prepared to forget it if they are.

Errol Flynn

I want a one-armed economist so that the guy could never make a statement and then say 'on the other hand ...'

Harry Truman

Don't get excited about a tax cut. It's like a mugger giving you back fare for a taxi.

Arnold Glasow

Money isn't everything, but it's a long way ahead of what comes next.

Edmund Stockdale

Here is a useful shopping tip: you can get a pair of shoes for £1 at bowling alleys.

Al Clethen

I get so tired of listening to one million dollars here, one million dollars there. It's so petty.

Imelda Marcos

I have never known an auctioneer to lie, unless it was absolutely necessary.

Josh Billings

There are three ways to lose money: on horses, women and engineers. Horses are the easiest, women the most fun and engineers the fastest.

Rolf Skar

A breakfast meeting is the most uncivilised idea I've ever heard of. If you're going to have a breakfast meeting it should be in bed with a beautiful woman.

Gordon White

Fire the whole purchasing department. They'd hire Einstein and then turn down his requisition for a blackboard.

Robert Townsend

I put the *Financial Times* on the floor and called my dog William over to pee on it. Wherever there was a mark I could do some trading.

Bob Beckman

All the great economic ills the world has known this century can be directly traced back to the London School of Economics.

N.M. Perrera

A billion here, a billion there and pretty soon you're talking about real money.

Everett Dirksen

Making a speech on economics is a bit like pissing down your leg. It seems hot to you but never to anyone else.

Lyndon B. Johnson

I'd like to be rich enough so I could throw soap away after the letters are worn off.

Andy Rooney

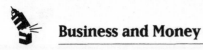

I was a lousy accountant. I always figured that if you came within eight bucks of what you needed you were doing OK. I made up the difference out of my own pocket.

Bob Newhart

My formula for success is rise early, work late, and strike oil.

Paul Getty

An economist's guess is as good as anybody else's.

Will Rogers

When I was young I used to think that wealth and power would bring me happiness. I was right.

Gahan Wilson

In the midst of life we are in debt.

Ethel Mumford

Women prefer men who have something tender about them – especially legal tender.

Kay Ingram

If all else fails, immortality can always be assured by a spectacular error.

J.K. Galbraith

My husband once worked for a company where they had a merit pay system. After six months they told him that he owed the company money.

Phyllis Diller

I am opposed to millionaires, but it would be dangerous to offer me the position.

Mark Twain

One way to solve all the traffic problems would be to keep all the cars that aren't paid for off the streets.

Will Rogers

I never pass an empty telephone box without pressing Button B. Button B has often been kind to me.

Joyce Cary

Avoid like the plague a clergyman who is also a business man.

Saint Jerome

I did not marry my wife because she had four million. I would have married her if she had only two million.

Charles Forte

One of the mysteries of human conduct is why adult men and women are ready to sign documents which they do not read, at the behest of salesmen they do not know, binding them to pay for articles they do not want, with money which they do not have.

Gerald Hurst

The best advice I was ever given was on my twenty-first birthday when my father said 'Son, here's a million dollars. Don't lose it'.

Larry Niven

Happiness is getting a bill you've already paid, so you can sit down and write a really nasty letter.

Peter Nero

My grandfather died in the great crash of 1929 – a stockbroker jumped out of a window and crushed him and his pushcart down below.

Mario Cuomo

The avoidance of taxes is the only intellectual pursuit that still carries any reward.

J.M. Keynes

Insufficient attention is given to real costs when installing university laboratory equipment. In some cases it would be cheaper not to install the equipment, but whenever it is needed to send each student in a separate chauffeur-driven Rolls-Royce to use the same equipment at another institution.

C.F. Carter

I'm very proud of my gold pocket watch. My grandfather, on his deathbed, sold me this watch.

Woody Allen

I worked my way up from nothing to a state of extreme poverty.

Groucho Marx

Those proud of keeping an orderly desk never know the thrill of finding something they thought they had irretrievably lost.

Helen Exley

I started out with nothing. I still have most of it.

Michael Davis

A good rule of thumb is if you've made it to thirty-five and your job still requires you to wear a name tag, you've probably made a serious vocational error.

Dennis Miller

It's so long since I've worked that one of my insurance stamps is worth more than a Penny Black.

Lenny Windsor

The three most beautiful words in the English language are 'find cheque enclosed'.

Dorothy Parker

Statistics show that women spend 85 per cent of the household budget, children 15 per cent and men the rest.

Lucille Goodyear

Drink and other Drugs

I am not a heavy drinker. I can sometimes go for hours
without touching a drop.

Noel Coward

I drink therefore I am.

W.C. Fields

If I had my life to live over again, I'd live over a saloon.

W.C. Fields

A woman drove me to drink – and I hadn't even the
courtesy to thank her.

W.C. Fields

I feel sorry for people who don't drink. They wake up in the
morning and that's the best they are going to feel all day.

Dean Martin

Some American writers who have known each other for
years have never met in the daytime or when both are sober.

James Thurber

An alcoholic is anyone you don't like who drinks more than
you do.

Dylan Thomas

You're not drunk if you can lie on the floor without holding
on.

Dean Martin

The drink in that pub is not fit for washing hearses.

Brendan Behan

Reality is an illusion created by a lack of alcohol.

N.F. Simpson

A tavern is a place where madness is sold by the bottle.

Jonathan Swift

May I suggest, sir, that if you want an impenetrable disguise for the fancy dress ball, that you go sober?

Samuel Foote

Work is the curse of the drinking classes.

Oscar Wilde

There are more old drunks than old doctors.

François Rabelais

My dad was the town drunk. Most of the time that's not so bad – but New York City?

Henny Youngman

I never drink water because of the disgusting things that fish do in it.

W.C. Fields

A cap of good acid costs five dollars and for that you can hear the Universal Symphony with God singing solo and the Holy Ghost on drums.

Hunter S. Thompson

I always keep a stimulant handy in case I see a snake – which I also keep handy.

W.C. Fields

He once had his toes amputated so he could stand closer to the bar.

Mike Harding

What contemptible scoundrel stole the cork from my lunch?

W.C. Fields

The trouble with him is that when he is not drunk he is sober.

W.B. Yeats

A debut is the first time a young girl is seen drunk in public.

F. Scott Fitzgerald

Cocaine is God's way of saying you're making too much money.

Robin Williams

I exercise strong self-control. I never drink anything stronger than gin before breakfast.

W.C. Fields

The AAAA is a new organisation for drunks who drive. Give them a call and they'll tow you away from the bar.

Martin Burden

Whiskey is by far the most popular of all the remedies that won't cure a cold.

Jerry Vale

The difference between a drunk and an alcoholic is that a drunk doesn't have to attend all those meetings.

Arthur J. Lewis

The Management of an Irish pub cannot be held responsible for any accidents which occur in the mad rush for the doors at closing time.

Tony Butler

A total abstainer is someone who abstains from everything except abstention.

Ambrose Bierce

Drink and other Drugs

He awoke with a severe hangover. His mouth felt as if it had been used as a latrine by some small animal.

Kingsley Amis

Your superego is that part of you which is soluble in alcohol.

Thomas L. Martin

I'd rather have a full bottle in front of me than a full frontal lobotomy.

Fred Allen

Perfection is such a nuisance that I often regret having cured myself of using tobacco.

Emile Zola

I once shook hands with Pat Boone and my whole right side sobered up.

Dean Martin

I can't die until the government finds a safe place to bury my liver.

Phil Harris

People keep warning me not to smoke too much, but I gotta. It's a matter of principle, like who's running my life – me or the *Reader's Digest*?

Dick Gregory

I got thrown out of Alcoholics Anonymous because when the other clients saw me they thought they were having the DTs.

Dave Dutton

There is nothing wrong with sobriety in moderation.

John Ciardi

Women add zest to the unlicenced hours.

Allen D. Thomas

Drink and other Drugs

A Temperance Hotel! You might as well speak of a celibate brothel.

George Tyrrell

Cocaine isn't habit forming. I should know because I've been taking it for years.

Tallulah Bankhead

I went into hospital for a liver transplant and boy was I unlucky! They gave me Oliver Reed's.

Lenny Windsor

My pappy told me never to bet my bladder against a brewery.

Lane Kirkland

The reason I drink is because when I'm sober I think I'm Eddie Fisher.

Dean Martin

Actually, it only takes one drink to get me drunk. The trouble is, I can't remember if it's the thirteenth or the fourteenth.

George Burns

I never smoked a cigarette until I was nine.

H.L. Mencken

You can tell German wine from vinegar by the label.

Mark Twain

It's not the taste of water I object to. It's the after effects.

Ronald Knox

I love drink, so long as it isn't in moderation.

Geoffrey Madan

Drink and other Drugs

I have been advised by the best medical authority, at my age, not to attempt to give up alcohol.

W.C. Fields

Never sit on a hard chair after drinking port.

H.J. Bidder

For a bad hangover take the juice of two quarts of whiskey.

Eddie Condon

Moonshine corn liquor has been known to stop the victim's watch, snap his suspenders and crack his glass eye right across.

Irvin Cobb

One day recently a man called out to me from the other side of the street asking me for the price of a drink. I beckoned him to come over for it and he waved me away. This has to be the Everest of laziness.

Jeffrey Bernard

I know I'm drinking myself to a slow death, but I'm in no hurry.

Robert Benchley

Wordsworth's standard of intoxication was miserably low.

J.H. Shorthouse

I distrust camels, and anyone else who can go a week without a drink.

Joe E. Lewis

If you drink, don't drive. Don't even putt.

Dean Martin

Health is what my friends are always drinking before they fall down.

Phyllis Diller

Drink and other Drugs

I smoke 10 to 15 cigars a day – at my age I have to hold on to something.

George Burns

There are just two reasons for drinking. One is when you are thirsty, to cure it; the other, when you are not thirsty, to prevent it.

Thomas Love Peacock

I used to do drugs. I got so wrecked one night, I waited for the stop sign to change – and it did.

Steve Krabitz

Education

'Whom are you?' he said, for he had been to night school.

George Ade

My problems all started with my early education. I went to a school for mentally disturbed teachers.

Woody Allen

Educational television should be absolutely forbidden. It can only lead to unreasonable disappointment when your child discovers that the letters of the alphabet do not leap up out of books and dance around with royal-blue chickens.

Fran Lebowitz

Anyone who has been to an English public school will always feel comparatively at home in prison.

Evelyn Waugh

I took a speed reading course and read *War and Peace* in twenty minutes. It's about Russia.

Woody Allen

I can speak Esperanto like a native.

Spike Milligan

I speak twelve languages – English is the bestest.

Stefan Bergman

My act is very educational. I heard a man leaving the other night saying 'Well, that's taught me a lesson.'

Ken Dodd

I wish that people who have difficulty in communicating would just shut up about it.

Tom Lehrer

If a man is a fool, you don't train him out of being a fool by sending him to university. You merely turn him into a trained fool, ten times more dangerous.

Desmond Bagley

'You will all write an essay on "self-indulgence". There will be a prize of half a crown for the longest essay, irrespective of any possible merit.' From then on all was silence until the break.

Evelyn Waugh

Never attribute to malice that which can be adequately explained by straightforward stupidity.

J.C. Collins

The average Ph.D thesis is nothing but the transference of bones from one graveyard to the other.

J.F. Dobie

An intellectual is someone who has found something more interesting than sex.

Edgar Wallace

A lecture is a process by which the notes of the professor become the notes of the students without passing through the minds of either.

R.K. Rathbun

Let me protest against recent attacks on the fagging system at public schools. In all my four years I can recall only eleven deaths from fagging.

J.B. Morton

A man who has never gone to school may steal from a freight car; but if he has a university education, he may steal the whole railroad.

Theodore Roosevelt

Dublin University contains the cream of Ireland – rich and thick.

Samuel Beckett

I expect you'll be becoming a schoolmaster, sir. That's what most of the gentlemen does, sir, that gets sent down for indecent behaviour.

Evelyn Waugh

I don't hold with bilingualism. English was good enough for Jesus Christ.

Ralph Melnyk

Violence is the repartee of the illiterate.

Alan Brien

I cheated in the final of my metaphysics examination. I looked into the soul of the boy sitting next to me.

Woody Allen

I acquired such skill in reading Latin and Greek that I could take a page of either, and distinguish which language it was by merely glancing at it.

Stephen Leacock

A college graduate returned home from his twenty-fifth class reunion and said to his wife – 'My classmates have all gotten so fat and bald they didn't even recognise me.'

Bennett Cerf

Trinity College Cambridge is like a dead body in a high state of putrefaction. The only interest is the worms that come out of it.

Lytton Strachey

Harvard is a storehouse of knowledge because the freshmen bring so much in and the graduates take so little out.

Charles W. Eliot

I used to keep my college roommate from reading my personal mail by hiding it in her textbooks.

Joan Welsh

The ablative absolute is an ancient form of grammatical error much admired by modern scholars.

Ambrose Bierce

We spend the first twelve months of our children's lives teaching them to walk and talk and the next twelve years telling them to sit down and shut up.

Phyllis Diller

Loaded firearms were strictly forbidden at St Trinians to all but Sixth Formers.

Timothy Shy

Ignorance is like a delicate exotic fruit; touch it and the bloom is gone.

Oscar Wilde

He can barely read and write – Eton, of course.

Lawrence Durrell

'Shut up', he explained.

Ring Lardner

When Lord Berners returned, many years later, to visit his old school, he was astonished to observe nothing but smiling faces – only to learn that it was a school no more and that the building was a lunatic asylum.

Arthur Marshall

He who can does – he who cannot, teaches.

George Bernard Shaw

In the first place God made idiots; that was for practice; then he made school boards.

Mark Twain

It is a pity that Chawser, who had geneyus, was so unedicated; he's the wuss speller I know of.

Artemus Ward

Sociology is the study of people who do not need to be studied by people who do.

E.S. Turner

When a woman becomes a scholar there is usually something wrong with her sexual organs.

Friedrich Nietzsche

There he goes – the man what learned me English.

J.B. Keane

Those who can – do. Those who cannot – teach. Those who cannot teach become deans.

Thomas L. Martin

You don't appreciate a lot of stuff in school until you get older. Little things like being spanked every day by a middle-aged woman – stuff you pay good money for in later life.

Emo Philips

I know you believe you understand what you think I said. But I am not sure you realise that what you heard is not what I meant.

Patrick Murray

As a major shareholder in a laxative company, I demand the abolition of examinations.

Patrick Murray

If you think education is expensive, try ignorance.

Derek Bok

Of course I know that 'knickers' begins with a 'k'. I've been to Oxford – it's one of the first things they teach you.

Alan Bennett

I understand that Harvard University is making its diplomas larger or smaller. I have forgotten which. This is a step in the right direction.

R.M. Hutchins

The only educational aspect of television is that it puts the repair-man's kids through college.

Joan Welsh

The full area of ignorance is not mapped; we are at present only exploring its fringes.

J.D. Bernal

When one day they opened a Catholic chapel, which was quickly followed by a pub, a block of shops and eventually a school. The school went up last because there was no profit in it.

Dominic Behan

When Scythrop grew up, he was sent, as usual, to a public school, where a little learning was painfully beaten into him, and from thence to the university, where it was carefully taken out of him; and he was sent home like a well-threshed ear of corn, with nothing in his head.

Thomas L. Peacock

Education

It is when the gods hate a man with uncommon abhorrence that they drive him into the profession of a schoolmaster.

Seneca

I was educated during the holidays from Eton.

Osbert Sitwell

One can always tell it is summer when one sees school-teachers hanging about the streets idly, looking like cannibals during a shortage of missionaries.

Robertson Davies

Teachers are overworked and underpaid. True, it is an exacting and exhausting business, this damming up the flood of human potentialities.

George B. Leonard

I won't say ours was a tough school, but we had our own coroner. We used to write essays like 'What I'm going to be if I grow up'.

Lenny Bruce

In our school you were searched for guns and knives on the way in and if you didn't have any, they gave you some.

Emo Philips

There is nothing on earth intended for innocent people, so horrible as a school. It is in some respects more cruel than a prison. In a prison for example, you are not forced to read books written by the warders and the governor.

George Bernard Shaw

The Royal Society is a collection of men who elect each other to office and then dine together at the expense of the society to praise each other over wine and award each other medals.

Charles Babbage

Education

In school we had a name for guys trying to get in touch with themselves.

P.J. O'Rourke

Like so many ageing college people, Pnin had long ceased to notice the existence of students on the campus.

Vladimir Nabokov

Education is the inculcation of the incomprehensible into the ignorant by the incompetent.

Josiah Stamp

I never lecture; not because I am shy or a bad speaker, but simply because I detest the sort of people who go to lectures and don't want to meet them.

H.L. Mencken

After spending four years as a college star he was a failure at pro football. All he had to show for it was an education.

Patrick Murray

In its fifty years of existence, all the Irish Institute for Advanced Studies has done is to show that there were two Saint Patricks and no God.

Patrick Murray

But, good gracious, you've got to educate him first. You can't expect a boy to be vicious till he's been to a good school.

H.H. Munro

I owe a lot to my teachers and mean to pay them back some day.

Stephen Leacock

When a teacher calls a boy by his entire name it means trouble.

Mark Twain

Education

My father wanted me to have all the educational
opportunities he never had, so he sent me to a girls' school.
Jack Herbert

I owe my great learning to the fact that I have always kept an
open book on my desk and read it whenever someone on
the phone said 'just a moment please'.
Helen Daley

You have to wonder about a country where the bombs are
smarter than the high school graduates. At least the bombs
can find Iraq on the map.
Whitney Brown

Food

Food

We lived for days on nothing but food and water.

W.C. Fields

Cucumber should be well sliced, dressed with pepper and vinegar, and then thrown out.

Samuel Johnson

If a lump of soot falls into the soup, and you cannot conveniently get it out, stir it well in, and it will give the soup a French taste.

Jonathan Swift

The cook was a good cook, as cooks go; and as cooks go, she went.

H.H. Munro

Cursed is he that uses peanuts when the recipe calls for almonds.

Christopher Driver

The secret of staying young is to live honestly, eat slowly and lie about your age.

Lucille Ball

Two sharks met and one said to the other 'My dear, I've discovered the most wonderful Italian restaurant. It's called the Andrea Doria.'

John Hollander

Eat at this restaurant and you'll never eat anywhere else again!

Bob Phillips

House-warming at Zola's – a very tasty dinner, including some grouse whose scented flesh Daudet compared to an old courtesan's flesh marinated in a bidet.

Edmond de Goncourt

I personally stay away from natural foods. At my age I need all the preservatives I can get.

George Burns

Americans will eat garbage provided you sprinkle it liberally with ketchup.

Henry Miller

Not alone is it quite acceptable to breast-feed in a restaurant, but it comes in quite handy when the waiter is late with the cream.

Blanche Knott

No one goes to that restaurant anymore – it's too crowded.

Yogi Berra

Whenever cannibals are on the brink of starvation, Heaven, in its infinite mercy, sends them a fat missionary.

Oscar Wilde

I'm at the age when food has taken the place of sex in my life. In fact, I've just had a mirror put over my kitchen table.

Rodney Dangerfield

I refuse to spend my life worrying about what I eat. There is no pleasure worth foregoing just for an extra three years in the geriatric ward.

John Mortimer

The most remarkable thing about my mother is that for thirty years she served the family nothing but leftovers. The original meal has never been found.

Calvin Trillin

I'm on a grapefruit diet. I eat everything except grapefruit.

Chi Chi Rodriguez

Is Elizabeth Taylor fat? Her favourite food is seconds.

Joan Rivers

Our trouble is that we drink too much tea. I see in this the slow revenge of the Orient, which has diverted the Yellow River down our throats.

J.B. Priestley

Ice-cream is exquisite – what a pity it isn't illegal.

Voltaire

Eat your vegetables and then you can have your dessert.

Laurence J. Peter

MacDonald's in Tokyo is a terrible revenge for Pearl Harbour.

S.I. Hayakawa

A gourmet who thinks of calories is like a tart who looks at her watch.

James Beard

Only Irish coffee provides in a single glass all four essential food groups: alcohol, caffeine, sugar and fat.

Alex Levine

Coffee in England always tastes like a chemistry experiment.

Agatha Christie

Tell the cook of this restaurant with my compliments that these are the very worst sandwiches in the whole world, and that, when I ask for a watercress sandwich, I do not mean a loaf with a field in the middle of it.

Oscar Wilde

I often take exercise. Why only yesterday I had breakfast in bed.

Oscar Wilde

I am not a vegetarian because I love animals; I'm a vegetarian because I hate plants.

A. W. Brown

To duplicate the taste of hammerhead shark, boil old newspapers in Sloan's Liniment.

Spike Milligan

For the chicken the egg demands involvement but for the pig bacon demands total commitment.

John A. Price

Hotel tea is when you have to mix together a plastic envelope containing too much sugar, a small plastic pot of something which is not milk but has curdled anyway, and a thin brown packet seemingly containing the ashes of a cremated mole.

Frank Muir

If you are ever at a loss to support a flagging conversation, introduce the subject of eating.

Leigh Hunt

Wearers of a Balliol tie enjoy a traditional immunity from cannibalism.

Lord Elton

In marital conflicts nothing should be thrown that is bigger than a bread box. Pie throwing is out of the question because if you bake like I do, a direct hit with one of those things could kill you.

Phyllis Diller

I have just given up spinach for Lent.

F. Scott Fitzgerald

Food

It is odd how all men develop the notion, as they grow older, that their mothers were wonderful cooks. I have yet to meet a man who will admit that his mother was a kitchen assassin and nearly poisoned him.

Robertson Davies

I bought all those Jane Fonda videos. I love to sit and eat cookies and watch them.

Dolly Parton

I could never learn to like her – except on a raft at sea with no other provisions in sight.

Mark Twain

The first law of dietetics seems to be: if it tastes good, it's bad for you.

Isaac Asimov

The worst thing that ever happened me was that I offered a fellow a crisp from my bag and he took two.

Vic Reeves

My wife does wonderful things with leftovers. She throws them out.

Herb Shriner

A food is not necessarily essential just because your child hates it.

Katharine Whitehorn

Food is an important part of a balanced diet.

Fran Lebowitz

Some breakfast food manufacturer hit upon the simple notion of emptying out the leavings of carthorse nosebags, adding a few other things like unconsumed portions of chicken layers mash, and the sweepings of racing stables, packing the mixture in little bags and selling them in health food shops.

Frank Muir

Nouvelle cuisine, roughly translated, means 'I can't believe I spent ninety-six dollars and I'm still hungry.'

Mike Kalin

Another good reducing exercise consists in placing both hands against the table edge and pushing back.

Robert Quillon

I will not eat oysters. I want my food dead. Not sick, not wounded, dead.

Woody Allen

I went on a diet, swore off drinking and heavy eating, and in fourteen days I lost two weeks.

Joe E. Lewis

Lawyers and other Professions

An actuary is someone who cannot stand the excitement of chartered accountancy.

Glan Thomas

Justice must not only be done, it must be seen to be believed.

J.B. Morton

I have nothing against undertakers personally. It's just that I wouldn't want one to bury my sister.

Jessica Mitford

Only lawyers and mental defectives are automatically exempt from jury duty.

George Bernard Shaw

When I came back to Dublin I was court-martialed in my absence and sentenced to death in my absence, so I said they could shoot me in my absence.

Brendan Behan

It's not the people who are in prison that worry me. It's the people who aren't.

Arthur Gore

A person guilty of rape should be castrated. That would stop him pretty quick.

Billy Graham

No brilliance is required in the law, just common sense and relatively clean fingernails.

John Mortimer

The thrill of hearing a jury return a guilty verdict is the ultimate sexual experience.

Judge Gregory Wallance

I am on record as saying that Simon Cameron would not steal a red-hot stove. I now wish to withdraw that statement.

Thaddeus Stevens

A lawyer is a learned gentleman who rescues your estate from your enemies and keeps it to himself.

Henry Brougham

Probably the only place where a man can feel really secure is in a maximum security prison, except for the imminent threat of release.

Germaine Greer

The court was not previously aware of the prisoner's many accomplishments. In view of these, we see fit to impose the death penalty.

Quentin Crisp

I went to see him hanged, drawn, and quartered, which was done, he looking as cheerful as any man could do in that condition.

Samuel Pepys

The only difference between doctors and lawyers is that lawyers merely rob you, whereas doctors rob you and kill you, too.

Anton Chekhov

Curiosity killed the cat, but for a while I was a suspect.

Steven Wright

Lawyers and other Professions

There are three reasons why lawyers are replacing rats as laboratory research animals. One is that they are plentiful, another is that the lab assistants don't get so attached to them and the third is that they will do things you just can't get rats to do.

Blanche Knott

My barber is an authority on everything except how to cut hair properly.

William H. Roylance

If once a man indulges himself in murder, very soon he comes to think very little of robbing; and from robbing he comes next to drinking and whistling on the Sabbath, and from that to incivility and procrastination. Once you begin upon this downward path you never know where you are to stop. Many a man has dated his ruin from some murder or other that perhaps he thought little of at that time.

Thomas de Quincey

Where there is no patrol car, there is no speed limit.

Petr Beckmann

A countryman between two lawyers is like a fish between two cats.

Benjamin Franklin

As repressed sadists are supposed to become policemen or butchers, so those with an irrational fear of life become publishers.

Cyril Connolly

If capital punishment was good enough for my father, it's good enough for me.

Victor Moore

A lawyer will do anything to win a case. Sometimes, he will even tell the truth.

Patrick Murray

The penalty for laughing in a courtroom is six months in jail – if it weren't for this penalty, the jury would never hear the evidence.

Bob Hope

I believe capital punishment to be an appropriate remedy for anyone who does me injury, but under no other circumstances.

F.L. Bailey

As one solicitor once wrote to another, 'Sir, I regret to inform you that there is danger of agreement breaking out between our respective clients.'

Reginald Hine

Death is not the end. There remains the litigation over the estate.

Ambrose Bierce

After a year in therapy, my psychiatrist said to me, 'Maybe life isn't for everyone.'

Larry Brown

Only one thing is impossible for God – to find any sense in any copyright law on the planet.

Mark Twain

The Scottish verdict 'not proven' means 'guilty, but don't do it again'.

Winifred Duke

An expert is one who knows so much about so little that he neither can be contradicted, nor is worth contradicting.

Henry Ward

Lawyers and other Professions

You can discourage burglars by wearing an old policeman's uniform and standing outside your house all day and night.

G. Byker

Why are there 12 jurors? Because there are 12 tribes of Israel, 12 months in a year, 12 inches in a foot, and 12 apostles.

Quentin Hogg

The right to pay fees to lawyers is a fundamental and ancient human right, and is at the kernel of what we know as democracy.

Flann O'Brien

1974 was the last time that Al Davis and I spoke without lawyers being paid.

Gene Klein

My definition of utter waste is a coachload of lawyers going over a cliff with three empty seats.

Lamar Hunt

Players like rules. If they didn't have any rules, they wouldn't have anything to break.

Lee Walls

I don't want a lawyer to tell me what I cannot do; I hire him to tell me how to do what I want to do.

J. P. Morgan

The most beautiful words in the English language are 'not guilty'.

Maxim Gorky

Under the English legal system, you are innocent until you are shown to be Irish.

Ted Whitehead

An incompetent lawyer can delay a trial for months or years.
A competent lawyer can delay one even longer.

Evelle J. Younger

Literature

Literature

I never read a book before reviewing it. I find that it just prejudices me.

Sydney Smith

Read over your compositions, and wherever you meet with a passage which you think is particularly fine, strike it out.

Samuel Johnson

The dawn is a term for the early morning used by poets and other people who don't have to get up.

Oliver Herford

He has produced a couplet. When our friend is delivered of a couplet, with infinite labour and pain, he takes to his bed, has straw laid down, the knocker tied up, and expects his friends to call and make enquiries.

Sydney Smith

Two people getting together to write a book is like three people getting together to have a baby. One of them is superfluous.

George Bernard Shaw

I never travel without my diary. One should always have something sensational to read in the train.

Oscar Wilde

My only claim to literary fame is that I used to deliver meat to a woman who became T. S. Eliot's mother-in-law.

Alan Bennett

If you want to get rich from writing, write the sort of thing that's read by persons who move their lips when they're reading to themselves.

Don Marquis

Literature

You may certainly not kiss the hand that wrote *Ulysses*. It's done lots of other things as well.

James Joyce

An editor should have a pimp for a brother so he can have someone to look up to.

Gene Fowler

Your manuscript is both good and original; but the part that is good is not original, and the part that is original is not good.

Samuel Johnson

Immature poets imitate; mature poets steal.

T.S. Eliot

This is not a book to be tossed aside lightly. It should be thrown with great force.

Dorothy Parker

I am sitting in the smallest room in the house. I have your review before me. It will soon be behind me.

Max Reger

I have been told by hospital authorities that more copies of my works are left behind by departing patients than those of any other author.

Robert Benchley

George Bernard Shaw writes like a Pakistani who has learned English when he was twelve years old to become a chartered accountant.

John Osborne

The Poems of Seth will be remembered long after those of Homer and Virgil are forgotten – but not until then.

Richard Porson

Literature

Reading Proust is like bathing in someone else's dirty water.
Alexander Woollcott

Finishing a book is just like you took a child out in the yard and shot it.

Truman Capote

For those who like this sort of thing, this is the sort of thing they will like.

Max Beerbohm

Donne's verses are like the peace and mercy of God. Like His peace, they pass all understanding, and like His mercy they seem to endure forever.

King James I

I was working on the proofs of one of my poems all day. In the morning I put a comma in and in the afternoon I took it back out again.

Oscar Wilde

Originality is undetected plagiarism.

W.R. Ince

Free verse is like playing tennis with the net down.
Robert Frost

I have read only one book in my life, and that is *White Fang*. It's so frightfully good I've never bothered to read another.
Nancy Mitford

There are two ways of disliking poetry. One way is to dislike it, and the other is to read Pope.

Oscar Wilde

Many thanks for your book – I shall lose no time in reading it.
Benjamin Disraeli

Warren Harding, the only man, woman, or child who ever wrote a simple declarative sentence with seven grammatical errors, is dead.

e.e. cummings

To me Poe's prose is unreadable – like Jane Austen's. No, there is a difference. I could read Poe's prose on a salary, but not Jane Austen's.

Mark Twain

Mr Irvin Cobb took me into his library and showed me his books, of which he has a complete set.

Ring Lardner

Mr Waugh is a parochial English writer (tautologies gush from my pen!)

Gore Vidal

Writers of thrillers tend to gravitate to the Secret Service as the mentally unstable become psychiatrists and the impotent become pornographers.

Malcolm Muggeridge

On the day when a young writer corrects his first proof sheets, he is as proud as a schoolboy who has just got his first dose of pox.

Charles Baudelaire

His books are going like wildfire – everybody is burning them.

George de Witt

I am addicted to literature. I never go anywhere without a Trollope.

Alec Guinness

Literature

Your function as a critic is to show that it is really you yourself who should have written the book, if you had had the time, and since you hadn't you are glad that someone else had, although obviously it might have been done better.

Stephen Potter

Shakespeare said pretty well everything and what he left out, James Joyce, with a nudge from meself, put in.

Brendan Behan

When I want to read a book, I write one.

Benjamin Disraeli

Paradise Lost is a book that, once put down, is very hard to pick up again.

Samuel Johnson

Oscar Wilde paraphrased and inverted the witticisms and epigrams of others. His method of literary piracy was on the lines of the robber Cacus, who dragged stolen cows backwards by the tails to his cavern so that their hoofprints might not lead to detection.

George Moore

This book of Italian literature shows a want of knowledge that must be the result of years of study.

Oscar Wilde

If you steal from one author, it's plagiarism; if you steal from many, it's research.

Wilson Mizner

I've given up reading books. I find it takes my mind off myself.

Oscar Wilde

Jeffrey Archer is proof of the proposition that in each of us there lurks a bad novel.

Julian Critchley

He was an author whose works were so little known as to be almost confidential.

Stanley Walker

There are just three rules for writing – but nobody knows what they are.

Somerset Maugham

G.K. Chesterton and Hilaire Belloc were the two buttocks of one bum.

T. Sturge Moore

This book is dedicated to the one woman fate created just for me. So far I've managed to avoid her.

Jon Winokur

Thomas Gray walks as if he had fouled his small-clothes, and looks as if he smelt it.

Christopher Smart

Perhaps the saddest lot that can befall mortal man is to be the husband of a lady poet.

George Jean Nathan

George Sand was a great cow-full of ink.

Gustave Flaubert

My brother-in-law wrote an unusual murder story. The victim got killed by a man from another book.

Robert Sylvester

Nobody ever went broke underestimating the taste of the American public.

H.L. Mencken

It is wrong to lecture on a living poet. One performs autopsies only on corpses.

Robert Graves

I always read the last page of a book first so that if I die before I finish I'll know how it turned out.

Nora Ephron

A publisher would as soon see a burglar in his office as a poet.

H. de Vere Stacpoole

Most of today's books have an air of having been written in one day from books read the night before.

N.S. Chamfort

If you can't annoy somebody there is little point in writing.

Kingsley Amis

God created the poet, then took a handful of the rubbish that was left and made three critics.

T.J. Thomas

When in doubt, ascribe all quotations to George Bernard Shaw.

Nigel Rees

Nature, not content with denying him the art of thinking, conferred on him the gift of writing.

George Bernard Shaw

James, why don't you write books that people can read?

Nora Joyce

Before they made S.J. Perelman they broke the mould.
Groucho Marx

The censorious said that she slept in a hammock and
understood Yeats's poems but her family denied both stories.
H.H. Munro

It is a mean thief or a successful author who plunders the dead.
Austin O'Malley

Waldo is one of those people who would be enormously
improved by death.
H.H. Munro

Shaw is the spinster aunt of English literature.
Kenneth Tynan

The author of this novel and all the characters mentioned in
it are fictitious. There is no such city as Manchester.
Howard Spring

Concerning no subject would Shaw be deterred by the
minor accident of total ignorance from penning a definitive
opinion.
Roger Scruton

She is so unreadable that people will finally believe her to be
a classic.
Ernest Hemingway

This is the sixth book I've written, which isn't bad for a guy
who has only read two.
George Burns

Every word that Lillian Hellman writes is a lie, including
'and' and 'the'.
Mary McCarthy

I can forgive Alfred Nobel for having invented dynamite, but only a fiend in human form could have invented the Nobel Prize.

George Bernard Shaw

There is no greater bliss in life than when the plumber eventually comes to unblock your drains. No writer can give that sort of pleasure.

Victoria Glendinning

It took twelve years to undo the harm caused by Housman's lecture on poetry.

I.A. Richards

Robert Bridges's anthology, *The Spirit of Man*, is like a vomit after a rich meal.

A.C. Benson

Mr C.L. Dodgson neither claims nor acknowledges any connection with any pseudonym or with any book not published under his own name.

Lewis Carroll

I did so enjoy your book darling. Everything that everybody writes in it is so good.

Mrs Patrick Campbell

I would cheerfully pay George Bernard Shaw's funeral expenses at any time.

Henry Irving

In Ireland they try to make a cat clean by rubbing its nose in its own filth. James Joyce has tried the same treatment on the human subject. I hope it may prove successful.

George Bernard Shaw

Literature

We all know of course that women are habitually constipated, but to represent them in fiction as being altogether devoid of a back passage seems to me really an excess of chivalry.

Somerset Maugham

The preface is the most important part of a book. Even reviewers read a preface.

Philip Guedalla

A woman who writes commits two sins; she increases the number of books and decreases the number of women.

Alphonse Kerr

If we cannot stamp out literature in our own country, we can at least stop it being brought in from outside.

Evelyn Waugh

It was a book to kill time for those who like it better dead.

Rose Macaulay

I often quote myself. It adds spice to my conversation.

George Bernard Shaw

Now that I know I am about to die, all right then, I'll say it: Dante makes me sick.

L.F. de Vega Carpio

One should not be too severe on English novels; they are the only relaxation of the intellectually unemployed.

Oscar Wilde

Writing is easy. All you have to do is to stare at a blank piece of paper until drops of blood form on your forehead.

Gene Fowler

Literature

If a third of all the novelists and maybe two thirds of all the poets now writing dropped dead suddenly, the loss to literature would not be great.

Charles Osborne

Magazines all too frequently lead to books and should be regarded as the heavy petting of literature.

Fran Lebowitz

First coffee. Then a bowel movement. Then the muse joins me.

Gore Vidal

I thought I'd begin by reading a poem by Shakespeare, but then I thought 'why should I?' He never reads any of mine.

Spike Milligan

I am not feeling very well. I can only write prose today.

W.B. Yeats

The most important difference between poetry and any other branch of publishing is, that whereas with most categories of books you are aiming to make as much money as possible, with poetry you are aiming to lose as little as possible.

T.S. Eliot

Andiatorocte is the title of a volume of poems by the Rev. Clarence Walworth, of Albany N.Y. It is a word borrowed from the Indians, and should, we think, be returned to them as soon as possible.

Oscar Wilde

This erratum slip has been inserted by mistake.

Alasdair Gray

Literature

In America only the successful writer is important, in France all writers are important, in England no writer is important, and in Australia you have to explain what a writer is.

Geoffrey Cotterell

A good many young writers make the mistake of enclosing a stamped self-addressed envelope, big enough to send the manuscript back in. This is too much of a temptation for the editor.

Ring Lardner

Studying literature at Harvard is like learning about women at the Mayo Clinic.

Roy Blount

If a writer has to rob his mother, he will not hesitate; 'Ode to a Grecian Urn' is worth any number of old ladies.

William Faulkner

If I should die, think only this of me
That in some corner of a foreign field
There lies a plagiarist.

Derek Alder

He is a distinguished man of letters. He works for the Post Office.

Max Kaufmann

Dear Editor, What I have written you is a damn good story. If you have any comments, write them on the back of a cheque.

Erle Stanley Gardner

'The Ancient Mariner' would not have been so popular if it had been called 'The Old Sailor'.

Alan Coren

Living — Family and Relations

If you don't clean your house for two months it doesn't get any dirtier.

Quentin Crisp

Never go to bed mad – stay up and fight.

Phyllis Diller

The General was essentially a man of peace – except of course in his domestic affairs.

Oscar Wilde

Insanity is hereditary; you can get it from your children.

Sam Levenson

I love children. Especially when they cry – for then someone takes them away.

Nancy Mitford

It's better to be black than gay because when you're black you don't have to tell your mother.

Charles Pierce

Every time a child says 'I don't believe in fairies', there's a little fairy somewhere that falls down dead.

J.M. Barrie

Why should we do anything for posterity? What has posterity ever done for us?

Joseph Addison

Children really brighten up a household – they never turn the lights off.

Ralph Bus

I have never understood this liking for war. It panders to instincts already well catered for within the scope of any respectable domestic establishment.

Alan Bennett

Any astronomer can predict with absolute accuracy just where every star in the universe will be at 11.30 tonight. He can make no such prediction about his teenage daughter.

James T. Adams

Watching your daughter being collected by her date feels like handing over a million dollar Stradivarius to a gorilla.

Jim Bishop

My husband and I have decided to start a family while my parents are still young enough to look after them.

Rita Rudner

You cannot be happy with a woman who pronounces the first 'd' in Wednesday.

Peter de Vries

When I go to the beauty parlour, I always use the emergency entrance. Sometimes I just go for an estimate.

Phyllis Diller

Most women are not as young as they are painted.

Max Beerbohm

My aunt once sent me a postal order for five pounds for coming top of a list.

F. W. Abernathy

Have you ever had one of those days when you have had to murder a loved one because he is the devil?

Emo Philips

Another good thing about being poor is that when you are seventy your children will not have you declared legally insane in order to gain control of your estate.

Woody Allen

Your mother, sir, under the pretence of keeping a bawdy house, was in reality a receiver of stolen property.

Samuel Johnson

Some mornings it just doesn't seem worth it to gnaw through the leather straps.

Emo Philips

There are three stages of man: he believes in Santa Claus; he does not believe in Santa Claus; he is Santa Claus.

Bob Phillips

To watch a child drowning within a few yards of me has a dispiriting effect upon my appetite.

Harry Graham

The child was a keen bed-wetter.

Noel Coward

She invariably was first over the fence in the mad pursuit of culture.

George Ade

I never met a kid I liked.

W.C. Fields

Few misfortunes can befall a boy which bring worse consequences than to have a really affectionate mother.

Somerset Maugham

Anyone who hates children and animals can't be all bad.
W.C. Fields

I have good looking kids; thank goodness my wife cheats on me.

Rodney Dangerfield

The flashier kind of widow may insist on sleeping with only black men during the first year after the death.
P.J. O'Rourke

My folks first met on the subway trying to pick each other's pockets.

Freddie Prinze

I cannot tell you if genius is hereditary, because heaven has granted me no offspring.
James McNeill Whistler

He is like a mule, with neither pride of ancestry nor hope of posterity.
Robert G. Ingersoll

Whatever women do they must do twice as well as men to be thought half as good. Luckily, this is not difficult.
Charlotte Whitton

Even if your father had spent more of your mother's immoral earnings on your education you would still not be a gentleman.
Frank Otter

Last week I stated that this woman was the ugliest woman I had ever seen. I have since been visited by her sister and now wish to withdraw that statement.
Mark Twain

Living — Family and Relations

The best way to find something you have lost is to buy a replacement.

Ann Landers

I hate housework! You make the beds, you do the dishes – and six months later you have to start all over again.

Joan Rivers

There are three ages of man – youth, age, and 'you're looking wonderful'.

Francis Spellman

In general my children refuse to eat anything that hasn't danced on television.

Erma Bombeck

An extravagance is anything you buy that is of no earthly use to your wife.

Franklin P. Adams

Children nowadays are tyrants. They contradict their parents, gobble their food, and tyrannise their teachers.

Socrates (425 B.C.)

A genius is a man who can rewrap a new shirt and not have any pins left over.

Dino Levi

It was very good of God to let Thomas and Mrs Carlyle marry one another and so make only two people miserable instead of four.

Samuel Butler

Wealth is any income that is at least one hundred dollars a year more than the income of one's wife's sister's husband.

H.L. Mencken

All a child can expect is that its father be present at the conception.

Joe Orton

Having a family is like having a bowling alley installed in your head.

Martin Mull

I like children – fried.

W.C. Fields

There are only two things that a child will share willingly – communicable diseases and its mother's age.

Benjamin Spock

Man is not born free, he is attached to his mother by a cord and is not capable of looking after himself for at least seven years (seventy in some cases).

Katharine Whitehorn

I was much distressed by the next door people who had twin babies and played the violin; but one of the twins has died, and the other has eaten the fiddle – so all is peace.

Edward Lear

The baby is fine. The only problem is that he looks like Edward G. Robinson.

Woody Allen

My wife has a slight impediment in her speech – every now and then she stops to breathe.

Jimmy Durante

I have never got over the embarrassing fact that I was born in bed with a woman.

Wilson Mizner

Living — Family and Relations

She was one of those women who go through life demanding to see the manager.

G. Patrick

When you see a married couple coming down the street, the one who is two or three steps ahead is the one that's mad.

Helen Rowland

A lot of people would rather tour sewers than visit their cousins.

Jane Howard

I love mankind – it's people I can't stand.

Charles Schultz

Childhood is that wonderful time of life when all you need to do to lose weight is to take a bath.

Richard S. Zera

Alimony is like buying oats for a dead horse.

Louis A. Safian

To lose one parent may be regarded as a misfortune; to lose both looks like carelessness.

Oscar Wilde

The ultimate penalty for bigamy is two mothers-in-law.

George Russell

Retirement at sixty-five is ridiculous. When I was sixty-five I still had pimples.

George Burns

Leon Brittain looked like a bloke in the sixth form who never had a date.

Simon Hoggart

I don't feel old – I don't feel anything until noon. Then it's time for my nap.

Bob Hope

When I was a boy, the Dead Sea was only sick.

George Burns

Why a four year old child could understand this report. Run out and find me a four year old child. I can't make head nor tail out of it.

Groucho Marx

Every day, in every way, I get worse and worse.

Patrick Murray

He was watching the moon come up lazily out of the old cemetery in which nine of his daughters were lying, and only two of whom were dead.

James Thurber

Santa Claus has the right idea – visit people only once a year.

Victor Borge

Isn't it funny how everyone in favour of abortion has already been born?

Patrick Murray

No man who has wrestled with a self-adjusting card table can ever be quite the man he once was.

James Thurber

The main difference between an Essex girl and a supermarket trolley is that a supermarket trolley has a mind of its own.

Ray Leigh

I know I was cruel to other children because I remember stuffing their nostrils with putty, and beating a little boy with stinging nettles.

Vita Sackville-West

The real menace in dealing with a five year old is that in no time at all you begin to sound like a five year old.

Jean Kerr

When Lady Louise Moncrieff's sixteenth child was born, her sister was present and called out 'It's all right Louise, and you have got another little boy'. And the reply of the poor tired lady was 'My dear, I really don't care if it is a parrot'.

Lord Ormathwaite

I love to go to the playground and watch the children jumping up and down. They don't know I'm firing blanks.

Emo Philips

The male is a domestic animal which, if treated with firmness and kindness, can be trained to do most things.

Jilly Cooper

I'd love to slit my mother-in-law's corsets and watch her spread to death.

Phyllis Diller

You know you're getting old when you stoop to tie your shoes and wonder what else you can do while you're down there.

George Burns

I was the kid next door's imaginary friend.

Emo Philips

I am the only woman in the world who has her dresses rejected by the Salvation Army.

Phyllis Diller

The highlight of my childhood was making my brother laugh so hard the food came out of his nose.

Garrison Keillor

The worst sensation I know of is getting up at night and stepping on a toy train.

Kin Hubbard

My grandfather started walking five miles a day when he was sixty. Now he's eighty-five and we don't know where the hell he is.

Ellen de Generis

Two can live as cheaply as one, but it costs them twice as much.

Frank Sullivan

My parents warned me never to open the cellar door or I would see things I shouldn't see. So one day when they were out I did open the cellar door and I did see things I shouldn't see – grass, flowers, the sun ...

Emo Philips

Tell your nice mummies and daddies to buy this book for you and hit them until they do.

Spike Milligan

Distant relatives are the best kind and the further away the better.

Kin Hubbard

When you see what some girls marry, you realise how they must hate to work for a living.

Helen Rowland

I do wish I could tell you my age, but it is impossible. It keeps changing all the time.

Greer Garson

Children are the most desirable opponents at Scrabble as they are both easy to beat and fun to cheat.

Fran Lebowitz

The trouble with children is that they are not returnable.

Quentin Crisp

I took my mother-in-law to Madame Tussaud's Chamber of Horrors and one of the attendants said 'Keep her moving sir, we're stocktaking.'

Les Dawson

I'm at that age now where just putting my cigar in its holder is a thrill.

George Burns

One of the delights known to age and beyond the grasp of youth is that of *not going*.

J.B. Priestley

The one phrase it is imperative to know in every foreign language is 'my friend will pay'.

Alan Whicker

I've never struck a woman in my life – not even my own mother.

W.C. Fields

I cannot believe that out of 100,000 sperm, you were the quickest.

Steven Pearl

Reinhart was never his mother's favourite – and he was an only child.

Thomas Berger

Wild horses couldn't drag a secret out of most women. However, women seldom have lunch with wild horses.

Ivern Boyett

When a woman says, 'I don't wish to mention any names', it ain't necessary to mention any names.

Kin Hubbard

A Boy Scout troop is a lot of boys dressed as jerks, led by a jerk dressed as a boy.

Shelley Berman

Nowadays, they spend £10,000 for a school bus to pick the kids right up at the door so they don't have to walk. Then they spend £200,000 for a gym so they can get some exercise.

Red Blanchard

I'm very pleased to be here. Let's face it, at my age I'm very pleased to be anywhere.

George Burns

My mother didn't breast-feed me. She said she just liked me as a friend.

Rodney Dangerfield

Help a man in trouble and he'll never forget you – especially the next time he's in trouble.

Johnny Lyons

I have already given two cousins to the war and I am ready to sacrifice my wife's brother.

Artemus Ward

97

What ought to be done to the man who invented the celebrating of anniversaries? Mere killing would be too light.
Mark Twain

I have had more trouble with D.L. Moody than with any other man I ever met.
D.L. Moody

The woman who can sacrifice a clean unspoiled penny stamp is probably unborn.
H.H. Munro

Mother Nature is wonderful. She gives us twelve years to develop a love for our children before turning them into teenagers.
Eugene P. Bertin

I understand the importance of bondage between parent and child.
Dan Quayle

Friends are people who borrow books and set wet glasses on them.
E.A. Robinson

They say such nice things about people at their funerals that it makes me sad to realise that I'm going to miss mine by just a few days.
Garrison Keillor

Fraser left his children unbaptised – but his wife did it secretly in the washing basin.
Virginia Woolf

As Miss America, my goal is to bring peace to the entire world and then get my own apartment.
Jay Leno

Take a small boy smeared with honey and lower him between the walls. The bees will fasten themselves to him by the hundreds and can be scraped off when he is pulled up, after which the boy can be thrown away. If no small boy smeared with honey can be found, it may be necessary to take an ordinary small boy and smear him, which should be a pleasure.

S.J. Perelman

As he was lowering the body into its last resting place, the respected grave-digger suddenly collapsed and died, which event cast a gloom over the entire proceedings.

Bernard Falck

It takes forty dumb animals to make a fur coat, but only one to wear it.

Bryn Jones

I'm going home next week. It's a kind of emergency – my parents are coming here.

Rita Rudner

I think that husbands and wives should live in separate houses. If there's enough money, the children should live in a third.

Cloris Leachman

We never talked in our family. We communicated by putting Ann Landers articles on the fridge.

Judy Gold

My photographs do me an injustice. They look just like me.
Phyllis Diller

My grandmother was a very tough woman. She buried three husbands and two of them were just napping.

Rita Rudner

I have problems flown in fresh daily wherever I am.

Richard Lewis

People ask me what I'd most appreciate getting for my eighty-seventh birthday. I'll tell you: a paternity suit.

George Burns

When I was a girl I had only two friends, and they were imaginary. And they would only play with each other.

Rita Rudner

Until I was thirteen, I thought my name was 'shut up'.

Joe Namath

Happiness is having a large, loving, caring, close-knit family in another city.

George Burns

I am thirty years old, but I read at the thirty-four year old level.

Dana Carvey

When I was a boy of fourteen, my father was so ignorant I could hardly stand to have the old man around. But when I got to be twenty-one, I was astonished at how much he had learned in seven years.

Mark Twain

When I was a child, I wanted to be an invalid when I grew up.

Quentin Crisp

I don't plan to grow old gracefully. I plan to have face lifts until my ears meet.

Rita Rudner

Alimony is the curse of the working classes.

Norman Mailer

Somewhere on this earth, every ten seconds, a woman gives birth to a child. We must find this woman and stop her at once.

Sam Levenson

Never lend your car to anyone to whom you have given birth.

Erma Bombeck

At my age flowers scare me.

George Burns

Picasso was a delightful, kindly, friendly, simple little man. When I met him he was extremely excited and overjoyed because his mother-in-law had just died and he was looking forward to the funeral.

Edith Sitwell

Never put off until tomorrow what can be put off until the day after tomorrow just as well.

Mark Twain

Remember, blood is not only thicker than water, it's much more difficult to get off the carpet.

Phyllis Diller

My mother was like a sister to me, only we didn't have sex quite so often.

Emo Philips

One or two days before moving house, place your goldfish bowl in the freezer. When the time comes to move you will find that your fish can be transported in a car or van with no danger of spillage.

D.A. Roberts

If a man smiles in his own house, somebody is sure to ask him for money.

William Feather

Living — Family and Relations

Once, when somebody in our house stepped on the cat's paw, my mother turned to the cat and said sternly 'I told you not to go around barefoot!'

Zero Mostel

My mother-in-law had to stop skipping for exercise. It registered seven on the Richter Scale.

Les Dawson

Dahlia is my good and deserving aunt, not to be confused with Aunt Agatha, who eats broken bottles and wears barbed wire next to the skin.

P.G. Wodehouse

While your mother-in-law is alive, domestic peace is out of the question.

Juvenal

It is a singular fact that a month or two before his daughter's marriage, the father, the husband, the bread-winner, who has made the whole affair possible, is afflicted with imbecility – that is in the estimation of the female members of the tribe. They fuss and buzz about like a swarm of bees, arranging, planning, arguing, advising, whispering in corners, yelling over the telephone, buying this and ordering that. The only person never consulted, never allowed to open his mouth is Daddy, who 'doesn't understand'.

A.P. Herbert

There are two things in this life for which we are never fully prepared. Twins.

Josh Billings

To be a successful father there is one absolute rule: 'when you have a kid, don't look at it for the first two years'.

Ernest Hemingway

During the blitz I was asked if I wanted to have my books or my son evacuated to the safety of the country. I chose my books because many of them were irreplaceable but I could always have another son.

Evelyn Waugh

I was born in Lowell, Massachusetts, and the explanation is quite simple. I wished to be near my mother.

James McNeill Whistler

I am so busy I have had to put off the date of my death.

Bertrand Russell

I didn't hire Scott as assistant coach because he's my son. I hired him because I'm married to his mother.

Frank Layden

For the parent of a Little Leaguer, a baseball game is simply a nervous breakdown divided into innings.

Earl Wilson

I owe a lot to my parents – especially my mother and father.

Greg Norman

Teenagers, are you tired of being harassed by your stupid parents? Act now. Move out, get a job, and pay your own bills – while you still know everything.

John Hinde

Adam was the luckiest man in the world – he had no mother-in-law.

Sholom Aleichem

I have just returned from a children's party. I am one of the survivors. There are not many of us.

Percy French

There are three ways to get something done; do it yourself, hire someone, or forbid your kids to do it.

Mona Crane

On the plus side, death is one of the few things that can be done as easily lying down.

Woody Allen

My uncle Sammy was an angry man. He had printed on his tombstone 'What are you looking at?'

Margaret Smith

Never raise a hand to your kids. It leaves your groin unprotected.

Red Buttons

My father never took me to the zoo. He said if they want me they will come and get me.

Rodney Dangerfield

When you are in trouble, people who call to sympathise, are really only looking for more details.

Edgar W. Howe

Love, Sex, Marriage, Men and Women

He said it was artificial respiration, but now I find that I am to have his child.

Anthony Burgess

Sara could commit adultery at one end and weep for her sins at the other, and enjoy both operations at once.

Joyce Cary

Sex without love is an empty experience, but as empty experiences go, it's a pretty good empty experience.

Woody Allen

All this fuss about sleeping together. For physical pleasure I'd sooner go to my dentist any day.

Evelyn Waugh

It's so long since I've had sex I've forgotten who ties up whom.

Joan Rivers

The world is full of people who are ready to think the worst when they see a man sneaking out of the wrong bedroom in the middle of the night.

Will Cuppy

The majority of husbands remind me of an orangutang trying to play the violin.

Honoré de Balzac

It is well to write love letters. There are certain things it is not easy to ask your mistress for face to face – like money for instance.

Henri de Regnier

In the circles in which I move, sleeping with a woman does not constitute an introduction.

Virginia McLeod

I thought men like that shot themselves.

King George V

The quickest way to a man's heart is through his chest.

Roseanne Barr

If it wasn't for pickpockets and frisking at airports I wouldn't have any sex life at all.

Rodney Dangerfield

A lady is a woman who never shows her underwear unintentionally.

Lillian Day

I'm such a good lover because I practise a lot on my own.

Woody Allen

A eunuch is a man who has had his works cut out for him.

Robert Byrne

His designs were strictly honourable; that is to rob a lady of her fortune by way of marriage.

Henry Fielding

Sex between a man and a woman can be wonderful – provided you get between the right man and the right woman.

Woody Allen

What a blonde – she was enough to make a bishop kick a hole in a stained glass window.

Raymond Chandler

I blame my mother for my poor sex life. All she told me was 'the man goes on top and the woman underneath'. For three years my husband and I slept in bunk beds.

Joan Rivers

Love, Sex, Marriage...

The Love Bird is one hundred per cent faithful to his mate –
as long as they are locked together in the same cage.

Will Cuppy

There is nothing in the world like the devotion of a married
woman. It's a thing no married man knows anything about.

Oscar Wilde

I'd marry again if I found a man who had fifteen million
dollars, would sign over half of it to me before the marriage,
and guarantee he'd be dead within a year.

Bette Davis

Women are like elephants – everyone likes to look at them
but no one likes to have to keep one.

W.C. Fields

My best birth control now is to leave the lights on.

Joan Rivers

Happiness is watching TV at your girlfriend's house during a
power failure.

Bob Hope

Oh Lord, give me chastity, but do not give it yet.

St Augustine

She was so ugly she could make a mule back away from an
oat bin.

Will Rogers

Divorce is the sacrament of adultery.

Jean Guichard

What would men be without women? Scarce, sir, mighty
scarce.

Mark Twain

Niagara Falls is the bride's second great disappointment.
Oscar Wilde

My love life is terrible. The last time I was inside a woman
was when I visited the Statue of Liberty.
Woody Allen

How I wish that Adam had died with all his ribs in his body.
Dion Boucicault

I was actually the first birth from an inflatable woman.
Tony de Meur

I would rather go to bed with Lillian Russell stark naked
than with Ulysses S. Grant in full military regalia.
Mark Twain

I think people should be free to engage in any sexual
practices they choose – they should draw the line at goats
though.
Elton John

A woman's mind is cleaner than a man's – that's because she
changes it more often.
Oliver Herford

A man ought not to marry without having studied anatomy,
and dissected at least one woman.
Honoré de Balzac

A man who marries his mistress creates a vacancy in the
position.
James Goldsmith

Sex is an act which on sober reflection one recalls with
repugnance and in a more elevated mood even with disgust.
A. Schopenhauer

The trees along the banks of the Royal Canal are more sinned against than sinning.

Patrick Kavanagh

My wife is the sort of woman who gives necrophilia a bad name.

Patrick Murray

It is bad manners to begin courting a widow before she gets home from the funeral.

Seumas MacManus

Drying a widow's tears is one of the most dangerous occupations known to man.

Dorothy Dix

Boy was my wife romantic! When I first met her she used to go round with a mattress strapped to her back.

Roy Brown

Marriage is like putting your hand into a bag of snakes in the hope of pulling out an eel.

Leonardo da Vinci

Sexual intercourse is a grossly overrated pastime; the position is undignified, the pleasure momentary and the consequences utterly damnable.

Lord Chesterfield

Every woman is entitled to a middle husband she can forget.

Adela Rogers St. Johns

I had bad luck with both my wives. The first one left me and the second one didn't.

Patrick Murray

I go from stool to stool in singles bars hoping to get lucky, but there's never any gum under any of them.

Emo Philips

Men and women, women and men. It will never work.

Erica Jong

When a man steals your wife, there is no better revenge than to let him keep her.

Sacha Guitry

So little time, so many beautiful women to make love to.

Arturo Toscanini

I am the only man in the world with a marriage licence made out 'to whom it may concern'.

Mickey Rooney

Women's intuition is the result of millions of years of not thinking.

Rupert Hughes

My wife and I pondered for a while whether to take a vacation or get a divorce. We decided that a trip to Bermuda is over in two weeks, but a divorce is something you always have.

Woody Allen

Splendid couple – slept with both of them.

Maurice Bowra

Men are superior to women. For one thing, men can urinate from a speeding car.

Will Durst

I'm dating a woman now who, evidently, is unaware of the fact.

Garry Shandling

She was stark naked except for a PVC raincoat, dress, net stockings, undergarments, shoes, rain hat and gloves.

Keith Waterhouse

What is wrong with a little incest? It's both handy and cheap.

James Agate

I'm a wonderful housekeeper. Every time I get a divorce, I keep the house.

Zsa Zsa Gabor

She had once heard a semi-drunken peer say on TV that marriage without infidelity was like a salad without dressing.

Keith Waterhouse

Love is temporary insanity curable by marriage.

Ambrose Bierce

Love is the delusion that one woman differs from another.

H.L. Mencken

Bisexuality doubles your chances of a date on a Saturday night.

Woody Allen

Never make a task of pleasure, as the man said when he dug his wife's grave only three feet deep.

Seumas MacManus

It doesn't matter what you do in the bedroom as long as you don't do it in the streets and frighten the horses.

Mrs Patrick Campbell

She dresses to the left.

Patrick Murray

Love is the answer – but while you're waiting for the answer, sex raises some pretty good questions.

Woody Allen

My boyfriend and I broke up. He wanted to get married and I didn't want him to.

Rita Rudner

Ten men waiting for me at the door? Send one of them home, I'm tired.

Mae West

My wife is a sex object – every time I ask for sex, she objects.

Les Dawson

When a woman behaves like a man, why doesn't she behave like a nice man?

Edith Evans

A successful man is one who makes more money than his wife can spend. A successful woman is one who can find such a man.

Lana Turner

The people I'm furious with are the women's liberationists. They keep getting up on soapboxes and proclaiming women are brighter than men. That's true, but it should be kept quiet or it ruins the whole racket.

Anita Loos

There are only about twenty murders a year in London and not all are serious – some are just husbands killing their wives.

G.H. Hatherill

Sending your girl's love letters to your rival after he has married her is one form of revenge.

Ambrose Bierce

I sold the memoirs of my sex life to a publisher – they are going to make a board game out of it.

Woody Allen

He kissed me as though he was trying to clear the drains.

Alida Baxter

My wife Mary and I have been married for forty-seven years and not once have we had an argument serious enough to consider divorce; murder, yes, but divorce, never.

Jack Benny

Some women's idea of being faithful is not having more than one man in bed at the same time.

Frederic Raphael

The main difference between men and women is that men are lunatics and women are idiots.

Rebecca West

Basically my wife was immature. I'd be at home in my bath and she'd come in and sink my boats.

Woody Allen

I've been married six months. She looks like a million dollars, but she only knows a hundred and twenty words and she's only got two ideas in her head. The other one is hats.

Eric Linklater

Love is just a dirty trick played on us to achieve the continuation of the species.

Somerset Maugham

A terrible thing happened to me last night again – nothing.

Phyllis Diller

I married beneath me. All women do.

Nancy Astor

I chased a woman for almost two years only to discover her tastes were exactly like mine – we were both crazy about girls.

Groucho Marx

Here's to woman! Would that we could fall into her arms without falling into her hands.

Ambrose Bierce

She said he proposed something on their wedding night that even her own brother wouldn't have suggested.

James Thurber

I like George and Harriet Grote. I like him; he's so lady-like. And I like her; she's such a perfect gentleman.

Sydney Smith

The chain of wedlock is so heavy that it takes two to carry it, sometimes three.

Alexandre Dumas

The ideal marriage consists of a deaf husband and a blind wife.

Padraig Colum

Every man should have the opportunity of sleeping with Elizabeth Taylor – and at the rate she's going, every man will.

Nicky Hilton

A nymphomaniac is a woman as obsessed with sex as the average man.

Mignon McLaughlin

My wife is as cold as the hairs on a polar bear's bum.

Les Dawson

It was so cold I almost got married.

Shelley Winters

We had gay burglars the other night. They broke in and rearranged the furniture.

Robin Williams

Despite my thirty years of research into the feminine soul, I have not yet been able to answer the great question that has never been answered: What does a woman want?

Sigmund Freud

It is impossible to obtain a conviction for sodomy from an English jury. Half of them don't believe that it can physically be done, and the other half are doing it.

Winston Churchill

Women should have labels on their foreheads saying 'Government Health Warning: women can seriously damage your brains, genitals, current account, confidence, razor blades, and good standing among your friends'.

Jeffrey Bernard

You can lead a horticulture but you can't make her think.

Dorothy Parker

Sex is just poor man's polo.

Clifford Odets

I don't see so much of Alfred any more since he got so interested in sex.

Mrs Alfred Kinsey

Marriage is a ghastly public confession of a strictly private intention.

Ian Hay

If a pretty back view won't let you catch it up, it has probably got a horrible face.

Sydney Tremayne

If there is reincarnation, I'd like to come back as Warren Beatty's fingertips.

Woody Allen

Mankind and woman unkind.

Dick Diabolus

Lady Capricorn, he understood, was still keeping open bed.

Aldous Huxley

You know, of course, that the Tasmanians, who never committed adultery, are now extinct.

Somerset Maugham

All this divorce – when I meet a man now the first thing I think about is 'Is this the sort of man I want my children to spend their weekends with?'

Rita Rudner

There is one thing I would break up over, and that is if she caught me with another woman. I wouldn't stand for that.

Steve Martin

I kissed my first woman and smoked my first cigarette on the same day: I have never had time for tobacco since.

Arturo Toscanini

If God had intended us to be nudists we would have been born with no clothes on.

Leonard Lyons

Sex is the invention of a very clever venereal disease.

David Cronenberg

When a woman, in the company of two men, addresses herself almost exclusively to one, you may be sure that she is busy beneath the table pressing the foot of the other.

Gian-Carlo Menotti

I am always looking for meaningful one-night stands.

Dudley Moore

I never understood what he saw in her until I saw her eating corn on the cob at the Caprice.

Coral Browne

It is not good for man to be alone. But oh my God, what a relief.

John Barrymore

There are a number of mechanical devices which increase sexual arousal, particularly in women. Chief among these is the Mercedes-Benz 380SL convertible.

P.J. O'Rourke

I wrote out a little list of questions for Pierre to put to the Pope about our marriage problems.

Margaret Trudeau

I'll come to your room at five o'clock. If I'm late, start without me.

Tallulah Bankhead

I can't for the life of me understand why people keep insisting that marriage is doomed. All five of mine worked out.

Peter de Vries

A woman is only a woman, but a good cigar is a smoke.

Rudyard Kipling

A woman without a man is like a fish without a bicycle.
Gloria Steinem

The happiest time of anyone's life is just after the first divorce.

J.K. Galbraith

Adultery? Why fool about with hamburger when you can have steak at home?

Paul Newman

I'm at the stage of life when if a girl says 'no' to me I'm profoundly grateful to her.

Woody Allen

There is nothing wrong with making love with the light on. Just make sure the car door is closed.

George Burns

She broke up with me when she found out I was sleeping with her.

Brian McCormick

Burt Reynolds once asked me to go out with him. I was in his room at the time.

Phyllis Diller

Love is a matter of chemistry – sex is simply physics.
G.M. Mark

She smoked 120 gaspers per day, swore like a fisherman, drank like a fish, and was promiscuous with men, women and Etonians.

Quentin Crisp

If you are bored with your present enemies and want to make some new ones, tell two of your women friends that they look alike.

Mignon McLaughlin

I once read an advertisement in a woman's magazine that went something like this:
Do you want him to remember you and think of you when you're not there? Always wear the same perfume when you go out with him. The sense of smell is one of the greatest memory prodders. He'll learn to associate that scent with you and think of you every time he smells it, even on someone else.
My God, does the woman think I'm a Labrador retriever?

Gilbert Harding

I have been to a funeral. I cannot describe to you the howl which the widow set up at proper intervals.

Charles Lamb

By all means marry; if you get a good wife, you'll become happy; if you get a bad one, you'll become a philosopher.

Socrates

Even if man could understand women he still wouldn't believe it.

A. W. Brown

Women now have the right to plant rolled-up dollar bills in the jockstraps of steroid-sodden male strippers.

Howard Ogden

I have never married – I find that if I come to like a young woman well enough to marry her, I also find that I have come to like her far too well to wish to see her tied to an irritable bad-tempered old boor for life.

Gilbert Harding

Sex is God's joke on human beings.

Bette Davis

Making love to Marilyn Monroe was like kissing Hitler.

Tony Curtis

My ultimate fantasy is to entice a man to my bedroom, put a gun to his head, and say 'make babies or die'.

Ruby Wax

Condemned female murderers get sheaves of offers of marriage.

George Bernard Shaw

My notion of a wife at forty is that a man should be able to change her, like a bank note, for two twenties.

Douglas Jerrold

Women are an alien race of pagans set down among us. Every seduction is a conversion.

John Updike

I have climbed the ladder of success, wrong by wrong.

Mae West

Basically I wanted a woman who was an economist in the kitchen and a whore in bed. I wound up with a woman who was a whore in the kitchen and an economist in bed.

Geoffrey Gorer

Men come of age at sixty, women at fifteen.

James Stephens

I've been in love with the same woman for forty years – if my wife ever finds out, she'll kill me.

Henny Youngman

A misogynist is a man who hates women as much as women hate each other.

H.L. Mencken

Men of every age flocked around Diana Cooper like gulls round a council tip.

John Carey

A woman's most erogenous zone is her mind.

Raquel Welch

I bequeath my entire estate to my wife on condition that she marries again. I want to be sure that there will be at least one man who will regret my death.

Heinrich Heine

Sorry Mr Frost, I sleep only with the first eleven.

Antonia Fraser

I blame my father for telling me about the birds and the bees. I was going steady with a woodpecker for two years.

Bob Hope

Why should I get married and make one woman happy when I can stay single and make hundreds happy?

Frederick Lonsdale

You may be wondering what a map of the trade winds of the North Atlantic is doing on page 134 of a book entitled *Is Sex Necessary?* We realise that in most books on sex page 134 contains a cut away cross-section of the female anatomy. In our opinion a map of the trade winds of the North Atlantic is equally useful in understanding women.

James Thurber

It was a perfect marriage – she didn't want to and he couldn't.

Spike Milligan

I would read *Playboy Magazine* more often, but my glasses keep steaming over.

George Burns

Always get married early in the morning. That way, if it doesn't work out, you haven't wasted a whole day.

Mickey Rooney

I'm not taking my wife with me to Paris because you don't take a sausage roll to a banquet.

Winston Churchill

Life is a sexually transmitted disease and the mortality rate is one hundred per cent.

R.D. Laing

I said to my husband, 'you must develop some mechanical skills, like getting out of bed'.

Phyllis Diller

Homosexuality is Nature's attempt to get rid of the soft boys by sterilising them.

F. Scott Fitzgerald

I know nothing about sex because I was always married.

Zsa Zsa Gabor

A woman's place is in the wrong.

James Thurber

A woman is like a tea bag. You can't tell how strong she is until you put her in hot water.

Nancy Reagan

My wife and I had a fight the other night. Nothing much – just two police cars.

Henny Youngman

My parents had only one argument in forty-five years. It lasted forty-three years.

Cathy Ladman

The most difficult year of marriage is the one you're in.

Franklin P. Jones

Doris Day is as wholesome as a bowl of cornflakes and at least as sexy.

Dwight MacDonald

I am a double bagger. Not alone does my husband put a bag over my face when we are making love but he also puts a bag over his own head in case my bag should fall off and he should have to look at me.

Joan Rivers

The height of ingratitude is the failure of Reno to erect a monument to Henry the Eighth.

Gerald F. Lieberman

That woman speaks eighteen languages and she can't say 'No' in any of them.

Dorothy Parker

An Arab and his camel are inseparable. It has been said that an Arab would give up his wife rather than give up his camel. Personally I haven't got a camel, but I think it's a great idea.

Groucho Marx

No man living knows more about women than I do – and I know nothing.

Seymour Hicks

Mr Ball? How very singular.

Thomas Beecham

I feel like a million tonight – but one at a time.

Mae West

Her grief lasted longer than I have known any widow's – three days.

Joseph Addison

I was with this girl the other night and from the way she was responding to my skillful caresses, you would have sworn she was conscious from the top of her head to the tag on her toes.

Emo Philips

It has been discovered experimentally that you can draw laughter from an audience anywhere in the world, of any class or race, simply by walking on to a stage, and uttering the words 'I am a married man'.

Ted Kavanagh

Philosophy is to the real world as masturbation is to sex.

Karl Marx

Of course prostitutes have babies – where do you think traffic wardens come from?

Dave Dutton

I have everything I had twenty years ago – except that now it's all lower.

Gypsy Rose Lee

I found a long grey hair on Kevin's jacket last night. If it's another woman's I'll kill him. If it's mine I'll kill myself.

Neil Simon

The reproduction of mankind is a great marvel and mystery. Had God consulted me in the matter, I should have advised Him to continue the generation of the species by fashioning them of clay.

Martin Luther

I'm not really a homosexual – I just help them out when they're busy.

Frank Carson

Girls are always running through my mind. They don't dare walk.

Andy Gibb

It was a man's world – then Eve arrived.

Richard Armour

Her eyes were bright brown – like a couple of cockroaches desperately swimming in two saucers of boiled rhubarb.

Gerald Kersh

I know a lot of people didn't expect our relationship to last – but we've just celebrated our two months anniversary.

Britt Eckland

My wife and I had words – but I never got to use mine.

Fibber McGee

She was a really bad-looking girl. Facially, she resembled Louis Armstrong's voice.

Woody Allen

If you want to know how old a woman is, ask her sister-in-law.

Edgar W. Howe

Sex at the age of eighty-four is a wonderful experience –
especially the one in winter.

Milton Berle

A man is only as old as the women he feels.

Groucho Marx

Where would man be today if it weren't for women? In the
Garden of Eden eating watermelon and taking it easy.

C. Kennedy

It's too bad that in most marriage ceremonies they don't use
the word 'obey' any more. It used to lend a little humour to
the occasion.

Lloyd Cory

Marry her! Impossible! You mean a part of her; he could not
marry her all himself. There is enough of her to furnish
wives for a whole parish. You might people a colony with
her; or give an assembly with her; or perhaps take your
morning's walk round her, always provided there were
frequent resting-places, and you were in rude health.

Sydney Smith

Women have a much better time than men in this world.
There are far more things forbidden to them.

Oscar Wilde

Recently, I've ventured into the mammal family – so that's
good for my sex life.

Emo Philips

I wouldn't trust my husband with a young woman for five
minutes, and he's been dead for twenty-five years.

Kathleen Behan

People in a temper often say a lot of silly things that they really mean.

Penelope Gilliat

I shrug my shoulders in despair at women who moan at the lack of opportunities and then take two weeks off as a result of falling out with their boyfriends.

Sophie Mirman

It should be a very happy marriage – they are both so in love with him.

Irene Thomas

The nearest I've been to a sexual experience lately is finding lipstick on a cafe cup.

Guy Bellamy

I have so little sex appeal my gynaecologist calls me 'sir'.

Joan Rivers

It had always seemed to Louis that a fundamental desire to take postal courses was being sublimated by other people into sexual activity.

Malcolm Bradbury

If I had been a woman I would be constantly pregnant because I simply cannot say no.

Robert Maxwell

My classmates would copulate with anything that moved, but I never saw any reason to limit myself.

Emo Philips

I do not believe in using women in combat, because females are too fierce.

Margaret Mead

Marriage is a great institution, but I'm not ready for an institution yet.

Mae West

If feminists were really serious about the movement, they would do something about their poor sisters who are forced to live on large alimony handouts from men they simply can't stand.

Lloyd Cory

When I have one foot in the grave, I will tell the whole truth about women. I shall tell it, jump into my coffin, pull the lid over me, and say 'Do what you like now.'

Leo Tolstoy

My love life is so bad I'm taking part in the world celibacy championships. I meet the Pope in the semi-finals.

Guy Bellamy

I once had a large gay following, but I ducked into an alleyway and lost him.

Emo Philips

The only time my wife and I had a simultaneous orgasm was when the judge signed the divorce papers.

Woody Allen

It was a mixed marriage. I'm human, he was a Klingon.

Carol Leifer

I've married a few people I shouldn't have, but haven't we all?

Mamie Van Doren

I'm busier than a whore working two beds.

Edgar W. Howe

If he ever makes love to me and I get to hear about it, his life won't be worth living

Mae West

The only place men want depth in a woman is in her décolletage.

Zsa Zsa Gabor

Brains are never a handicap to a girl if she hides them under a see-through blouse.

Bobby Vinton

I have slept only with men I've been married to. How many women can make that claim?

Elizabeth Taylor

Some of the happiest marriages are when homosexuals marry upper-class ladies. The sex works, because the upper-class woman doesn't expect much, and the man just shuts his eyes and thinks of Benjamin Britten.

Jilly Cooper

Love is ideal. Marriage is real. The confusion of the two shall never go unpunished.

J. W. von Goethe

The poor wish to be rich, the rich wish to be happy, the single wish to be married, and the married wish to be dead.

Ann Landers

Of those that were born as men, all that were cowardly and spent their life in wrongdoing were transformed at the second birth into women. Such is the origin of women and of all that is female.

Plato

Every man is thoroughly happy twice in his life: just after he
has met his first love, and just after he has left his last one.

H.L. Mencken

If you are married, it takes just one to make a quarrel.

Ogden Nash

I wanted to be a sex maniac but I failed the practical.

Robert Mitchum

As a young man I used to have four supple members and one
stiff one. Now I have four stiff and one supple.

Henri Duc d'Aumale

A woman gives a man just two happy days: the day he
marries her, and the day he buries her.

Hipponax

As a child of eight, Mr Trout had once kissed a girl of six
under the mistletoe at a Christmas party, but there his sex life
had come to an abrupt halt.

P.G. Wodehouse

The difference between divorce and legal separation is that a
legal separation gives a husband time to hide his money.

Johnny Carson

I was at a gay nineties party the other night. All the men
were gay and all the women were ninety.

Eric Morecambe

We sleep in separate rooms, we have dinner apart, we take
separate vacations. We're doing everything we can to keep
our marriage together.

Rodney Dangerfield

Women love men for their defects; if men have enough of them women will forgive them everything, even their gigantic intellects.

Oscar Wilde

When a couple decide to divorce, they should inform both sets of parents before having a party and telling all their friends. This is not only courteous but practical. Parents may be very willing to pitch in with comments, criticism and malicious gossip of their own to help the divorce along.

P.J. O'Rourke

I wasn't kissing your daughter, sir – I was just whispering in her mouth.

Chico Marx

Why does a woman work for ten years to change a man's habits and then complain that he's not the man she married?

Barbra Streisand

I like only two kinds of men – domestic and foreign.

Mae West

After we made love he took a piece of chalk and made an outline of my body.

Joan Rivers

One of my friends who is happily married has a husband so ugly she met him when a friend sent him over to her house to cure her hiccoughs.

Phyllis Diller

After my wife died, I put my mistress into cold storage for a bit.

H. G. Wells

When a man is a bit of a woman, one does like that bit to be a lady.

G.M. Young

We've just marked our tenth wedding anniversary on the calendar and threw darts at it.

Phyllis Diller

A husband should not insult his wife in public. He should insult her in the privacy of the home.

James Thurber

It takes a lot of experience for a girl to kiss like a beginner.

Joan Rivers

An open marriage is Nature's way of telling you that you need a divorce.

Ann Landers

What do I think of volkswagens? I've been in bigger women.

Harry Kurnitz

There is no bigger fan of the opposite sex than me, and I have the bills to prove it.

Alan J. Lerner

Dammit, sir, it is your duty to get married. You can't be always living for pleasure.

Oscar Wilde

Women who can, do. Those who can't become feminists.

Bobby Riggs

There is just one remark to which there is no answer – what are you doing with my wife?

Miguel de Cervantes

What part of 'no' don't you understand?

Rita Rudner

Not a soul dropped in to see me in my little cubicle in the office for days on end. I finally solved the problem by scratching my name off the door and replacing it with the legend Gents Room.

Dorothy Parker

To be able to turn a man out into the garden and tell him to stay there until the next meal, is every woman's dream.

Virginia Graham

When we got married my wife didn't have a rag on her back – but she's got plenty of them now.

Peter Eldin

Running after women never hurt anybody – it's catching them that does the damage.

Jack Davies

The great trick with a woman is to get rid of her while she thinks she's getting rid of you.

Soren Kierkegaard

All my wife has ever taken from the Mediterranean – from that whole vast intuitive culture – are four bottles of Chianti to make into lamps, and two china condiment donkeys named Sally and Peppy.

Peter Shaffer

Now that women are jockeys, baseball umpires, atomic scientists, and business executives, maybe someday they can master parallel parking.

Bill Vaughan

My wife's idea of double parking is to park her car on top of another car.

Shelley Berman

The longest sentence you can form with two words is 'I do'.

H.L. Mencken

She did have an illegitimate baby once but it was only a little one.

Frederick Marryat

Alas, she married another. They frequently do. I hope she is happy, because I am.

Artemus Ward

Be wary, how you marry one that hath cast her rider, I mean a widow.

James Howell

Almost any man can support the girl he marries, but the problem is – what's **he** going to live on?

Joseph Salak

When we want to read the deeds that are done for love, whither do we turn? To the murder columns.

George Bernard Shaw

Women are to be excluded from the eleventh annual conker championships at Oundle. Our event would be ridiculed if women competed.

Frank Elson

She could very well pass for forty-three, in the dusk with a light behind her.

W.S. Gilbert

Annette had never been in love, although she was not without experience. She had been deflowered at seventeen by a friend of her brother on the suggestion of the latter. Nicholas would have arranged it when she was sixteen, only he needed her just then for a black mass.

Iris Murdoch

I have no time for sex. It gets in the way of the action.

Alistair MacLean

Never trust a husband too far, nor a bachelor too near.

Helen Rowland

I've never yet turned over a fig leaf that didn't have a price tag on the other side.

Saul Bellow

If you never want to see a man again say 'I love you, I want to marry you, I want to have children'. They leave skid marks.

Rita Rudner

Every good painter who aspires to the creation of genuine masterpieces should first of all marry my wife.

Salvador Dali

A woman waits motionless until she is wooed. That is how the spider waits for the fly.

George Bernard Shaw

Love is the delightful interval between meeting a girl and discovering she looks like a haddock.

John Barrymore

I never knew what real happiness was until I got married. And by then it was too late.

Max Kauffmann

Wives are people who think it's against the law not to answer the phone when it rings.

Ring Lardner

My fiancé and I are having a little disagreement. What I want is a big church wedding with bridesmaids and flowers and a no-expense-spared reception; and what he wants is to break off our engagement.

Sally Poplin

'Tis better to have loved and lost.

Alfred Tennyson

The biggest myth is that as you grow older, you gradually lose your interest in sex. This myth probably got started because younger people seem to want to have sex with each other at every available opportunity including traffic lights, whereas older people are more likely to reserve their sexual activities for special occasions such as the installation of a new Pope.

Dave Barry

This is good news; of memory, hearing, all the faculties – the last to leave us is sexual desire and the ability to make love. That means that long after we're wearing bifocals or hearing aids, we'll be making love. But we won't know with whom or why.

Jack Paar

A promiscuous person is someone who is getting more sex than you are.

Victor Lownes

Men who don't understand women fall into two groups – bachelors and husbands.

Jacques Languirand

A Casanova provides a useful special service – the best women like Rolls Royces should be delivered to the customer fully run-in.

Jilly Cooper

My wife – God bless her – was in labour for thirty-two hours, and I was faithful to her the entire time.

Jonathan Katz

Divorce is painful. There's an easy way to save yourself a lot of trouble. Just find a woman you hate and buy her a house.

Pat Paulsen

Outside every thin woman is a fat woman trying to get in.

Katharine Whitehorn

If it's wet dry it. If it's dry wet it. Congratulations, you are now a gynaecologist.

Patrick Murray

She wore a low but futile décolletage.

Dorothy Parker

Anybody who says he can see through women is missing a lot.

Groucho Marx

I'm an intensely shy and vulnerable woman. My husband Norm has never seen me naked. Nor has he ever expressed the least desire to do so.

Dame Edna Everage

Media and Films

There is more joy in the newspaper world over one sinner who cuts his sweetheart's throat than over the ninety-nine just men who marry and live happily ever after.

A.P. Herbert

Television is called a medium because it is neither rare nor well done.

Ernie Kovacs

Television is very educational – every time it comes on I go into another room and read a book.

Groucho Marx

I knew Doris Day before she was a virgin.

Groucho Marx

I have a television set in every room of the house but one. There has to be some place you can go when Bob Monkhouse is on.

Benny Hill

An editor is one who separates the wheat from the chaff and prints the chaff.

Adlai Stevenson

A starlet is any girl under thirty in Hollywood who is not regularly employed in a brothel.

Ben Hecht

Dead? With the newspaper strike on, I wouldn't even consider it.

Bette Davis

Everything you read in the newspapers is absolutely true, except for that rare story of which you happen to have first-hand knowledge, which is absolutely false.

Erwin Knoll

In a mere half-century, films have gone from silent to
unspeakable.

Doug Larson

There is no bad publicity, except an obituary notice.

Brendan Behan

Television is a device that permits people who haven't
anything to do to watch people who can't do anything.

Fred Allen

Hollywood is an asylum run by the inmates.

Laurence Stallings

He had been kicked in the head by a mule when young, and
believed everything he read in the papers.

George Ade

'Hello', he lied.

Robert Maxwell

They shot too many pictures and not enough actors.

Walter Winchell

To give an accurate and exhaustive account of that period
would need a far less brilliant pen than mine.

Max Beerbohm

The reason why so many people showed up at Louis B.
Mayer's funeral was because they wanted to make sure he
was dead.

Samuel Goldwyn

Accuracy to a newspaper is what virtue is to a lady, except
that a newspaper can always print a retraction.

Adlai Stevenson

A publisher would prefer to see a burglar in his office to a poet.
Don Marquis

I was photographed on one occasion, sitting up in an over-elaborate bed looking like a heavily doped Chinese illusionist.

Noel Coward

One watches David Frost with the same mixture of fascination and disgust that one looks at one's turds floating in a toilet.

Patrick Murray

Sir, I have tested your gramophone machine. It adds a new terror to life and makes death a long-felt want.
Herbert Beerbohm Tree

Television is totally in the hands of semi-articulate barbarians who can barely read an autocue.

William Rushton

After being turned down by numerous publishers, he decided to write for posterity.

George Ade

If you cannot get a job as a pianist in a brothel, you become a royal reporter.

Max Hastings

We have all passed a lot of water since then.

Samuel Goldwyn

The essence of humour is surprise; that is why you laugh when you see a joke in *Punch*.

A. P. Herbert

Now Barabbas was a publisher.

Kenneth Tynan

Barbara Cartland's eyes were twin miracles of mascara and looked like two small crows that had crashed into a chalk cliff.

Clive James

What do you mean 'we' paleface?

Tonto

Television is for appearing on, not looking at.

Noel Coward

Films should have a beginning, a middle and an end – but not necessarily in that order.

Jean-Luc Godard

Glenda Jackson has a face to launch a thousand dredgers.

Jack de Manio

I don't write for pornographic magazines or swim in sewers.

Jerry Falwell

I am about to, or I am going to die. Either expression is used.

Noah Webster

Before television, people didn't even know what a headache looked like.

D. Fields

Never argue with a man who buys ink by the gallon.

Bill Greener

The current Hollywood outbreak of rabies is due to Hedda Hopper going round biting dogs.

Edith Sitwell

I have recently been broadcasting in the interests of a breakfast food whose name for the moment escapes me.

Alexander Woollcott

The only time I use women in films is when they're either naked or dead.

Joel Silver

Never let that son of a bitch in the studio again – until we need him.

Samuel Goldwyn

I love British cinema like a doctor loves his dying patient.

Ben Kingsley

Television is still in its infancy – that's why you have to get up and change it so often.

Michael Hynes

Hollywood is a trip through a sewer in a glass-bottomed boat.

Wilson Mizner

An epic is a movie with Charlton Heston in it.

James Agate

Otto Preminger couldn't direct his little nephew to the bathroom.

Dyan Cannon

No passion in the world, no love or hate, is equal to the passion to alter someone else's copy.

H. G. Wells

My films won't send people out into the streets with axes or anything. The Shirley Temple movies are more likely to do that. After listening to *The Good Ship Lollipop*, you just gotta go out and beat up somebody. Stands to reason.

Lee Marvin

What we want is a story that starts with an earthquake and works its way up to a climax.

Samuel Goldwyn

I don't want any yes-men around me. I want everyone to tell me the truth even if it costs them their jobs.

Samuel Goldwyn

We're overpaying him but he's worth it.

Samuel Goldwyn

You can fool all of the people all of the time if the advertising is right and the budget is big enough.

Joseph E. Levine

Some are born great, some achieve greatness, and some hire public relations officers.

Daniel J. Boorstin

Imagine the Lone Ranger's surprise when many years later he discovered that 'kemo sabay' means 'horse's ass'.

Garry Larsen

Beaverbrook is so pleased to be in Government that he is like the town tart who has finally married the Mayor.

Beverley Baxter

Having the critics praise you is like having the hangman say you've got a pretty neck.

Eli Wallach

Freedom of the press is limited to those who own a newspaper.

A.J. Liebling

Being published by the Oxford University Press is rather like being married to a duchess; the honour is greater than the pleasure.

G.M. Young

Most of the time Marlon Brando sounds as if he has a mouth full of wet toilet paper.

Rex Reed

Television is a twenty-one-inch prison. I'm delighted with it because it used to be that films were the lowest form of art. Now we have something to look down on.

Billy Wilder

David Frost is the bubonic plagiarist.

Jonathan Miller

No good will come of television. The word is half Greek and half Latin.

C.P. Scott

About once a month, after dinner, I gird up my loins such as they are, take as deep a breath as I can, throw my shoulders back as far as they will go, walk into the room with the television set, boldly turn it on, picking a channel at random, and then see how long I can stand it.

James Thurber

I have a face like an elephant's behind.

Charles Laughton

I saw the sequel to the movie *Clones* and you know what? It was the same movie!

Jim Samuels

Mr Mencken has just entered a Trappist monastery in Kentucky and left strict instructions that no mail was to be forwarded. The enclosed is returned, therefore, for your archives.

H.L. Mencken

Small earthquake in Chile – not many dead.

Claud Cockburn

My movies were the kind they show in prisons and aeroplanes, because nobody can leave.

Burt Reynolds

She would be a nymphomaniac if only they could calm her down a little.

Judy Garland

The longest word in the English language is the one which follows the phrase, 'And now, a word from our sponsor.'

Hal Eaton

Every time I sell 100,000 copies of *For Whom The Bell Tolls* I will forgive a son of a bitch, and when we sell a million I will forgive Max Eastman.

Ernest Hemingway

In Hollywood, writers are considered only the first drafts of human beings.

Frank Deford

You can take all the sincerity in Hollywood, place it in the navel of a fruitfly and still have room for three caraway seeds and a producer's heart.

Fred Allen

Paint eyeballs on my eyelids and I'll sleepwalk through any picture.

Robert Mitchum

I won't eat anything that has intelligent life, but I'll gladly eat a network executive or a politician.

Marty Feldman

Jack Warner has oilcloth pockets so he can steal soup.

Wilson Mizner

Awards are like haemorrhoids; sooner or later every asshole gets some.

Frederic Raphael

Lord Beaverbrook looked like a doctor struck off the roll for performing an illegal operation.

G.M. Young

The only work I ever turned down was a cable programme called *Diving for Excrement*.

Emo Philips

I've done my bit for motion pictures – I've stopped making them.

Liberace

It's greater than a masterpiece – why it's mediocre.

Samuel Goldwyn

I'll believe in colour television when I see it in black and white.

Samuel Goldwyn

Jack Benny lived on a diet of fingernails and coffee.

May Livingstone

Hollywood is Californication.

James Montgomery

The Royal Variety performance has taken on a geriatric air. People you assumed were dead totter on the stage to wild applause.

Richard Ingrams

Reading someone else's newspaper is like sleeping with someone else's wife. Nothing seems to be precisely in the right place, and when you find what you are looking for, it is not clear then how to respond to it.

Malcolm Bradbury

If I made Cinderella, the audience would be looking out for a body in the coach.

Alfred Hitchcock

Hollywood is Disneyland staged by Dante. You imagine purgatory is like this except that the parking is not so good.

Robin Williams

A reporter is a man who has renounced everything in life except the world, the flesh, and the devil.

David Murray

I improve on misquotation.

Cary Grant

Jogging is for people who aren't intelligent enough to watch Breakfast Television.

Victoria Wood

I once received a letter from a mother ambitious for her daughter. It read: 'I have a perfectly beautiful daughter. She is seventeen years old, five feet three inches tall, and weighs eight stone. Do you think she might succeed in films?' I replied 'Madam, it would be impossible to say, as you did not state her width'.

Alfred Hitchcock

Media and Films

Hitler's original title for *Mein Kampf* was *Four and a half Years of Struggle against Lies, Stupidity and Cowardice*. Everyone needs an editor.

Tim Foote

The *Sun* and the *Mirror* have become the standard-bearers of illiteracy.

Emyr Humphreys

Only presidents, editors and people with tapeworm have the right to use the editorial 'we'.

Mark Twain

Gentlemen, I agree with you that Napoleon is a tyrant, a monster, the sworn foe of our nation. But, gentlemen – he once shot a publisher.

Thomas Campbell

Take an idiot man from a lunatic asylum and marry him to an idiot woman, and the fourth generation of the connection should be a good publisher from an American point of view.

Mark Twain

Authors should write one novel and then be put in the gas chamber.

John P. Marquand

In Los Angeles they don't throw their garbage away. They make it into television shows.

Woody Allen

Tell me, how did you love my picture?

Samuel Goldwyn

For three days after death, hair and fingernails continue to grow but phone calls taper off.

Johnny Carson

If you're a sporting star, you're a sporting star. If you don't quite make it, you become a coach. If you can't coach, you become a journalist. If you can't spell, you introduce Grandstand on a Saturday afternoon.

Desmond Lynam

Clark Gable – if you said 'Clark, how are you' he was stuck for an answer.

Ava Gardner

The only memorable character in Kubrick's films over the past twenty years is Hal the computer.

Pauline Kael

Medicine and Doctors

I have the body of an eighteen year old. I keep it in the fridge.

Spike Milligan

I was under the care of a couple of medical students who couldn't diagnose a decapitation.

Jeffrey Bernard

The art of medicine consists in amusing the patient while Nature affects the cure.

Voltaire

Kilbarrack, over by Howth, my father always maintained, was the healthiest graveyard in the country, with the sea air.

Brendan Behan

Either this man is dead or my watch is stopped.

Groucho Marx

A sure cure for seasickness is to sit under a tree.

Spike Milligan

A shin is a device for finding furniture in the dark.

Colin Bowles

I'm not feeling very well – I need a doctor immediately. Ring the nearest golf course.

Groucho Marx

The operation was a complete success, but the patient died of something else.

John Chiene

Armpits lead lives of quiet perspiration.

Patrick Murray

Is there anything worn under the kilt? No, it's all in perfect working order.

Spike Milligan

My doctor gave me six months to live, but when I couldn't pay the bill he gave me six months more.

Walter Matthau

He wrote a doctor's hand – the hand which from the beginning of time has been so disastrous to the pharmacist and so profitable to the undertaker.

Mark Twain

Doctors think a lot of patients are cured who have simply quit in disgust.

Don Herold

One of the most difficult things to contend with in a hospital is the assumption on the part of the staff that because you have lost your gall bladder you have also lost your mind.

Jean Kerr

I make it a rule never to smoke more than one cigar at a time.

Mark Twain

Ordinarily he was insane, but he had lucid moments when he was merely stupid.

Heinrich Heine

My army medical consisted of two questions (i) Have you got piles? (ii) Any insanity in the family? I answered yes to both and was accepted A1.

Spike Milligan

Medicine and Doctors

His low opinion of medical students sprang largely from the days when he had been reading Theology at Cambridge and, on his attempt to break up a noisy party of medicals late one night, he had been forcibly administered an enema of Guinness stout.

Richard Gordon

Insanity doesn't just run in our family – it practically gallops.

Cary Grant

Condoms aren't completely safe. A friend of mine was wearing one and got hit by a bus.

Bob Rubin

My brain – that's my second favourite organ.

Woody Allen

One finger in the throat and one in the rectum make a good diagnostician.

William Osler

Anyone who goes to a psychiatrist should have his head examined.

Samuel Goldwyn

All those people with wooden legs – it's pathetic, they're not fooling anyone.

Michael Redmond

I refuse to endure months of expensive humiliation from a psychoanalyst only to be told that at the age of four I was in love with my rocking-horse.

Noel Coward

My piles bleed for you.

Herbert Beerbohm Tree

Every man catches himself in the zipper of his fly once, and only once in his lifetime.

Walt Giachini

Roses are red, violets are blue
I'm schizophrenic, and so am I.

Frank Crow

Henry the Fourth's feet and armpits enjoyed an international reputation.

Aldous Huxley

A woman went to a plastic surgeon and asked him to make her like Bo Derek. He gave her a lobotomy.

Joan Rivers

It is a poor doctor who cannot prescribe an expensive cure for a rich patient.

Sydney Tremayne

I woke up the other morning and found that everything in my room had been replaced by an exact replica. So I rang my best friend and told him that everything in my room had been replaced by an exact replica. He said 'Do I know you?'

Steven Wright

My father had a profound influence on me – he was a lunatic.

Spike Milligan

She got her looks from her father – he's a plastic surgeon.

Groucho Marx

I have just learnt about his illness; let us hope it is nothing trivial.

Irvin Cobb

Medicine and Doctors

Medicine is my lawful wife, literature is my mistress. When I get tired of one, I spend the night with the other. It is disorderly but it isn't dull and neither of them loses anything from my infidelity.

Anton Chekhov

My psychiatrist and I have decided that when we both think I am ready, I'm going to get in my car and drive off a bridge.

Neil Simon

Before undergoing a surgical operation, arrange your temporal affairs – you may live.

Ambrose Bierce

Everyone should have a few bad habits so he'll have something he can give up if his health fails.

Franklin P. Jones

I gave up visiting my psychoanalyst because he was meddling too much in my private life.

Tennessee Williams

The best medical speciality is dermatology. Your patients never call you out in the middle of the night, they never die of the disease, and they never get any better.

Martin H. Fischer

He has been a doctor a year now and has had two patients, no, three, I think – yes it was three; I attended their funerals.

Mark Twain

When I take up assassination, I shall start with the surgeons in this city and work up to the gutter.

Dylan Thomas

A paranoid is a man who knows a little of what is going on.

William Burroughs

I have finally come to the conclusion, that a good reliable set of bowels is worth more to a man than any quantity of brains.

Josh Billings

Happiness is nothing more than health and a poor memory.
Albert Schweitzer

Tell her she can't be allowed to die in peace – it's against the rules of the hospital.

John Fisher Murray

My father invented a cure for which there was no known disease – unfortunately my mother caught the cure and died of it.

Victor Borge

Dying is a very dull dreary affair, and my advice to you is to have nothing to do with it.

Somerset Maugham

My advice if you insist on slimming – eat as much as you like, just don't swallow it.

Harry Secombe

Our doctor would never really operate unless it was absolutely necessary. He was just that way. If he didn't need the money, he wouldn't lay a hand on you.

Herb Shriner

A psychiatrist is a man who asks you a lot of expensive questions your wife asks you for nothing.

Sam Bardell

Death is just nature's way of telling you to slow down.
Dick Sharples

Medicine and Doctors

Neurotic means he is not as sensible as I am, and psychotic means he's even worse than my brother-in-law.

Karl Menninger

A peptic ulcer is a hole in a man's stomach through which he crawls to escape from his wife.

J.A.D.Anderson

The first sign of his approaching end was when one of my old aunts, while undressing him, removed a toe with one of his socks.

Graham Greene

First you forget names, then you forget faces. Next you forget to pull your zipper up and finally you forget to pull it down.

George Burns

The medical student is likely to be the one son of the family too weak to labour on the farm, too indolent to do any exercise, too stupid for the bar and too immoral for the pulpit.

Daniel Gilman

The trouble with Freud is that he never played the Glasgow Empire Saturday night.

Ken Dodd

Modesty has ruined more kidneys than bad liquor.

S. Morris

We are all born mad. Some remain so.

Samuel Beckett

I have myself spent nine years in a lunatic asylum and have never suffered from the obsession of wanting to kill myself; but I know that each conversation with a psychiatrist in the morning made me want to hang myself because I knew I could not strangle him.

Antonin Artaud

Show me a sane man and I will cure him for you.

Carl Jung

Have you ever had the measles, and if so, how many?

Artemus Ward

What is a human being but an ingenious assembly of portable plumbing?

Christopher Morley

A psychiatrist is a man who goes to a strip-show to watch the audience.

Mervyn Stockwood

If a doctor treats your cold, it will go away in fourteen days. If you leave it alone, it will go away in two weeks.

Gloria Silverstein

I don't mind dying; the trouble is you feel so bloody stiff the next day.

George Axlerod

Are you all right? You should have two of everything down the sides and one of everything down the middle.

Ken Dodd

Doctors prescribe medicines of which they know little, to cure diseases of which they know less, in human beings of which they know nothing.

Voltaire

Running through the park I had a bad asthmatic attack –
three asthmatics jumped me. It was my own fault – I should
have heard them hiding.

Emo Philips

Psychoanalysis is the disease it purports to cure.

Karl Kraus

I was a caesarean birth but you can't really tell, except that
every time I leave the house I go out by the window.

Steven Wright

I didn't know the full facts of life until I was seventeen. My
father never talked about his work.

Martin Freud

Nature is that lovely lady to whom we owe polio, leprosy,
smallpox, syphilis, tuberculosis and cancer.

Stanley N. Cohen

A male gynaecologist is like an auto mechanic who has
never owned a car.

Carrie Snow

William Wilde, father of Oscar Wilde and a noted eye
specialist, operated on the father of George Bernard Shaw to
correct a squint, and overdid the correction so much that the
unfortunate man squinted the other way for the rest of his life.

Hesketh Pearson

Among the side effects of this drug, the most significant is
the immediate death of the patient.

Philip Mason

Exercise is bunk. If you are healthy, you don't need it; if you
are sick, you shouldn't take it.

Henry Ford

Medicine and Doctors

The trouble with heart disease is that the first symptom is often hard to deal with – sudden death.

Michael Phelps

I'm not crazy, but I think everyone else is.

Peter O'Toole

The only parts left of my original body are my elbows.

Phyllis Diller

Just because you are paranoid doesn't mean they aren't out to get you.

Patrick Murray

Jumping into the sea is a certain cure for seasickness.

John Ruskin

The great art of a quack is to time his imposture.

Richard Duppa

He is alive, but only in the sense that he cannot be legally buried.

Geoffrey Madan

The nicest present I ever got was an exploding suppository.

Emo Philips

One out of four people is mentally unbalanced. Think of your three closest friends. If they seem OK then you're the one.

Ann Landers

There must be something to acupuncture – after all, you never see any sick porcupines.

Bob Goddard

There are more men than women in mental hospitals which just goes to show who's driving who crazy.

Peter Veale

I slept well only once in my life, and even then I dreamt I was awake.

Irving Berlin

Happiness is a warm bed pan.

Christopher Hudson

A good patient is one who, having found a good doctor, sticks to him until he dies.

Oliver Wendell Holmes

Knocked down a doctor? With an ambulance? How could she? It's a contradiction in terms.

N.F. Simpson

There's another advantage of being poor – a doctor will cure you faster.

Kin Hubbard

One would think that in an age of unemployed doctors, the British Medical Association might support the noble art of boxing on the grounds that it provides more work for them. Instead they have voted to ban the sport altogether.

Auberon Waugh

Cyclists represent only one per cent of the traffic, but they account for ten per cent of the traffic deaths. We physicians call cyclists 'organ donors'.

Cheryl Winchell

I've lost six pounds on the way to the Super Bowl. Mind you, that's like throwing a deck chair off the Queen Mary.

Bill Parcells

Medicine and Doctors

When I meet a man whose name I cannot remember, I give myself two minutes, then if it is a hopeless case I always say 'And how is the old complaint?'

Benjamin Disraeli

While quacks normally kill you, doctors merely allow you to die.

Jean de la Bruyere

My dear doctor, I'm surprised to hear you say that I am coughing very badly, because I have been practising all night.

John Philpot Curran

Poor old Lord Mortlake, who had only two topics of conversation, his gout and his wife. I never could quite make out which of the two he was talking about.

Oscar Wilde

Except for an occasional heart attack I feel as young as I ever did.

Robert Benchley

The only weapon with which the unconscious patient can immediately retaliate upon the incompetent surgeon is the haemorrhage.

W.S. Halstead

Talk of the patience of Job, said a hospital nurse, Job was never on night duty.

Stephen Paget

The secret of longevity is to keep breathing.

Sophie Tucker

I've just had an operation for piles - all my troubles are behind me.

Ken Brett

He collected lists of fatal diseases and arranged them in alphabetical order so that he could put his finger without delay on any one he wanted to worry about.

Joseph Heller

I've already had medical attention – a dog licked me while I was on the ground.

Neil Simon

A successful doctor needs three things. A top hat to give him authority; a paunch to give him dignity, and piles to give him an anxious expression.

Samuel Johnson

A grave is a place where the dead are laid to await the coming of the medical student.

Ambrose Bierce

If your time hasn't come, not even a doctor can kill you.

M.A. Perlstein

There are three natural anaesthetics – sleep, fainting and death.

Oliver Wendell Holmes

Mr Anaesthetist, if the patient can stay awake, surely you can.

Wilfred Trotter

I have a perfect cure for a sore throat – cut it.

Alfred Hitchcock

I am always amazed to hear of air crash victims so badly mutilated that they have to be identified by their dental records. What I cannot understand is if they don't know who you are, how do they know who your dentist is?

Paul Merton

Music

The music teacher came twice a week to bridge the awful
gap between Dorothy and Chopin.

George Ade

The bagpipes are an instrument of torture consisting of a
leaky bag and punctured pipes, played by blowing up the bag
and placing the fingers over the wrong holes.

Dick Diabolus

Most rock journalism is people who cannot write
interviewing people who cannot talk for people who cannot
read.

Frank Zappa

Jazz is music invented for the torture of imbeciles.

Henry Van Dyke

I could eat alphabet soup and shit better lyrics than that.

Johnny Mercer

A violin is the revenge exacted by the intestines of a dead
cat.

Ambrose Bierce

The Mafia once moved in and took over the New York
Ballet. During a performance of 'Swan Lake', there was a lot
of money on the swan to live.

Woody Allen

Brass bands are all very well in their place – outdoors and
several miles away.

Thomas Beecham

Swans sing before they die – 'twere no bad thing did certain
persons die before they sing.

S. T. Coleridge

Classical music is the kind you keep thinking will turn into a tune.

Kin Hubbard

I have never heard any Stockhausen, but I do believe I have stepped in some.

Thomas Beecham

Wagner has some lovely moments but some terrible quarters of an hour.

Gioacchino Rossini

The harpsichord sounds like two skeletons copulating on a corrugated tin roof.

Thomas Beecham

She was a town-and-country soprano of the kind often used for augmenting grief at a funeral.

George Ade

The Sydney Opera House looks as if it were something that had crawled out of the sea and was up to no good.

Beverley Nichols

One cannot judge Wagner's opera Lohengrin after a first hearing and I have no intention of sitting through it a second time.

Gioacchino Rossini

Wagner's music is better than it sounds.

Mark Twain

Having adapted Beethoven's Ninth Symphony for *Fantasia*, Walt Disney commented 'Gee, this'll make Beethoven'.

Marshall McLuhan

Music

The third movement of Bartok's Fourth Quartet began with a dog howling at midnight, proceeded to imitate the regurgitations of the less refined type of water-closet and concluded with the cello reproducing the screech of an ungreased wheelbarrow.

Alan Dent

I find that distance lends enchantment to bagpipes.

William Blezard

Please do not shoot the pianist – he's doing his best.

Oscar Wilde

I liked your opera. I think I will set it to music.

Ludwig van Beethoven

I write music as a sow piddles.

W.A. Mozart

I'm a concert pianist. That's a pretentious way of saying I'm unemployed at the moment.

Oscar Levant

A highbrow is anyone who can listen to the William Tell Overture and not think of The Lone Ranger.

Jack Perlis

We will now have the Second Dance Rhapsody of Frederick Delius, a work which was given some years ago and of which we shall now hear the first performance.

Thomas Beecham

Wagner is the Puccini of music.

J.B. Morton

Why do we in England engage at our concerts so many third-rate continental conductors when we have so many second-rate ones of our own?

Thomas Beecham

It is sobering to consider that when Mozart was my age he had already been dead for a year.

Tom Lehrer

Bagpipes are the missing link between music and noise.

E.K. Kruger

Others, when the bagpipe sings i' the nose, cannot contain their urine.

William Shakespeare

If that's what the top twenty records sound like, I shudder to think what the bottom fifty must sound like.

C. Street

The third movement of Beethoven's Seventh Symphony is like a lot of yaks jumping about.

Thomas Beecham

Sleep is an excellent way of listening to an opera.

James Stephens

Crooning is a reprehensible form of singing that established itself in light entertainment mainly about the 1930s. It recommended itself at first to would-be singers without voices who were unable to acquire an adequate technique. The principle of crooning is to use as little voice as possible and instead to make a sentimental appeal by prolonged moaning somewhere near the written notes.

Eric Blom

Opera is when a guy gets stabbed in the back and instead of bleeding he sings.

Edward Gardner

Critics can't even make music by rubbing their back legs together.

Mel Brooks

Parsifal is the kind of opera that starts at 6 o'clock. After it has been going on for three hours you look at your watch and it says 6.20.

David Randolph

Mr Robin Day asks me to vouch for the fact that he can sing. I testify that the noise he makes is in fact something between that of a rat drowning, a lavatory flushing and a hyena devouring her after-birth in the Appalachian Mountains under a full moon.

Auberon Waugh

My favourite two composers are the Bachs – Johann Sebastian and Jacques Offen.

Victor Borge

The best tune of *Evita*, the already famous 'Don't Cry for me Argentina', is inferior as a melody to the ones I used when a boy to hear improvised on a saxophone outside the Albert Hall by a busker with only three fingers on his left hand.

Bernard Levin

There are seventy verses in the Uruguay national Anthem, which fact may account for the Uruguay standing army.

Franklin P. Adams

Anybody who has listened to certain kinds of music, or read certain kinds of poetry, or heard certain kinds of performances on the concertina, will admit that even suicide has its brighter aspects.

Stephen Leacock

If bullshit was music, that fellow would be a brass band.

Paddy Crosbie

After the United States premiere of *Salome*, the critics went up into the attic and dusted off adjectives that hadn't been in use since Ibsen was first produced in London. I remember that 'bestial', 'fetid', 'slimy', and 'nauseous' were among the more complimentary terms.

Deems Taylor

The inventor of the bagpipes was inspired when he saw a man carrying an indignant asthmatic pig under his arm. Unfortunately, the manmade sound never equalled the purity of the sound achieved by the pig.

Alfred Hitchcock

His Majesty does not know what the Grenadier Guards Band has just played, but it is never to be played again.

King George V

No operatic tenor has yet died soon enough for me.

Thomas Beecham

I wish the Government would put a tax on pianos for the incompetent.

Edith Sitwell

I don't like composers who think. It gets in the way of their plagiarism.

Howard Dietz

You made me love you, I didn't want to do it. You woke me up to do it.

Sammy Kahn

I have a very simple secret about playing the piano. I sit down on the piano stool and I make myself comfortable – and I always make sure that the lid over the keyboard is open before I start to play.

Artur Schnabel

'Spinning Wheel' by Blood, Sweat and Tears, is music to commit voluntary euthanasia by.

Simon Hoggart

If there is anyone here whom I have not insulted, I beg his pardon.

Johannes Brahms

You know what you do when you shit? Singing it's the same thing, only up!

Enrico Caruso

His vibrato sounded like he was driving a tractor over ploughed fields with weights tied to his scrotum.

Spike Milligan

The true gentleman is a man who knows how to play the bagpipes but doesn't.

Thomas Beecham

Bring not a bagpipe to a man in trouble.

Jonathan Swift

I knew a Russian peasant who could make his horse
micturate by whistling softly. That same whistling sound I
have heard in several pieces of electronic music, and it makes
me suffer the same desire as the horse.

Igor Stravinsky

When Phyllis Diller started to play, Steinway came down
personally and rubbed his name off the piano.

Bob Hope

You must play Chopin to me. The man with whom my wife
ran away played Chopin exquisitely.

Oscar Wilde

Last year I gave several lectures on 'Intelligence and the
appreciation of Music among Animals'. Today I am going to
speak to you about 'Intelligence and the appreciation of
Music among Critics.' The subjects are very similar.

Eric Satie

If there is music in hell it will be bagpipes.

Joe Tomelty

Modern music is the noise made by deluded speculators
picking through the slagpile.

Henry Pleasants

Schoenberg would be better off shovelling snow.

Richard Strauss

I like both kinds of music - country and western.

John Belushi

Music

Tchaikovsky thought of committing suicide for fear of being discovered as a homosexual, but today, if you are a composer and not a homosexual, you might as well put a bullet through your head.

Serge Diaghilev

Nationalities and Places

Nationalities and Places

In England there are a hundred religions and only one sauce which is melted butter.

Francesco Caracciolo

Note the tower, which is said to be the sixth highest in East Anglia.

Stephen Potter

Canada could have enjoyed English government, French culture and American know-how. Instead it ended up with English know-how, French government and American culture.

John Robert Colombo

The Irish gave the bagpipes to the Scots as a joke, but the Scots haven't seen the joke yet.

Oliver Herford

I am willing to love all mankind, except an American.

Samuel Johnson

People don't actually swim in Dublin Bay – they are merely going through the motions.

Brendan Behan

I would like to live in Manchester, England. The transition between Manchester and death would be unnoticeable.

Mark Twain

Always remember that you are an Englishman and therefore have drawn first prize in the lottery of life.

Cecil Rhodes

The first item on the agenda of every Irish organisation is 'The Split'.

Brendan Behan

It is no longer true that Continentals have a sex life whereas the English have hot-water bottles – the English now have electric blankets.

George Mikes

In Pierre Trudeau Canada has at last produced a political leader worthy of assassination.

Irving Layton

America is the only nation in history which miraculously has gone from barbarism to degeneracy without the usual interval of civilisation.

Georges Clemenceau

The bars in Dublin are shut from 2.30 to 3.30. We call it the Holy Hour. The politician who introduced it was shot an hour afterwards.

Brendan Behan

Once you've been on a plane full of drunken Australians doing wallaby imitations up and down the aisles, you'll never make fun of Americans again.

P.J. O'Rourke

The main difference between Los Angeles and yogurt is that yogurt has an active living culture.

Tom Taussik

There are still parts of Wales where the only concession to gaiety is a striped shroud.

Gwyn Thomas

Of course America had often been discovered before Columbus, but it had always been hushed up.

Oscar Wilde

For breakfast, the first morning I was in France, I had a
steaming bidet of coffee, followed by porridge and frogs.
Spike Milligan

The English have sex on the brain – which is a frightfully
uncomfortable place to have it.
Malcolm Muggeridge

In Paris they simply stared when I spoke to them in French; I
never did succeed in making those idiots understand their
own language.
Mark Twain

I have a great admiration for Mussolini, who has welded a
nation out of a collection of touts, blackmailers, ice-cream
vendors and gangsters.
Michael Bateman

The war situation has developed not necessarily to Japan's
advantage.
Emperor Hirohito (1945)

Much may be made of a Scotchman, if he be caught young.
Samuel Johnson

A great many people in Los Angeles are on strict diets that
restrict their intake of food. The reason for this appears to be
a widely-held belief that organically grown fruit and
vegetables make the cocaine work faster.
Fran Lebowitz

We must keep America whole and safe and unspoiled.
Al Capone

She lived in France – that country to which lesbianism is
what cricket is to England.
Quentin Crisp

America is the land of permanent waves and impermanent wives.

Brendan Behan

I know only two words of American slang; 'swell' and 'lousy'. I think 'swell' is lousy, but 'lousy' is swell.

J.B. Priestley

The high standards of Australians are due to the fact that their ancestors were all hand-picked by the best English judges.

Douglas Copland

I don't hold with abroad and think that foreigners speak English when our backs are turned.

Quentin Crisp

Those comfortably padded lunatic asylums which are known, euphemistically, as the stately homes of England.

Virginia Woolf

The noblest prospect which a Scotchman ever sees is the high road that leads him to England.

Samuel Johnson

There are over thirty words in the Irish language which are equivalent to the Spanish 'manana'. But somehow none of them conveys the same sense of urgency.

Patrick Kavanagh

When St Patrick drove the snakes out of Ireland, they swam to New York and joined the police force.

Eugene O'Neill

I have been trying all my life to like Scotchmen, and am obligated to desist from the experiment in despair.

Charles Lamb

Canada is useful only to provide me with furs.
Madame de Pompadour

Americans are a race of convicts and ought to be thankful
for anything we allow them short of hanging.
Samuel Johnson

No man is thoroughly miserable unless he is condemned to
live in Ireland.
Jonathan Swift

The English winter – ending in July, to recommence in August.
George Gordon

In Ireland a girl has the choice between perpetual virginity
and perpetual pregnancy.
George Moore

The French invented the only known cure for dandruff. It is
called the guillotine.
P. G. Wodehouse

Your proper child of Caledonia is the bandy-legged lout
from Tullietudlesleugh, who, after a childhood of intimacy
with the cesspool and the crablouse, and twelve months at
'the college' on moneys wrung from the diet of his family,
drops his threadbare kilt and comes south in a slop suit to
instruct the English in the arts of civilisation and in the
English language
T. W. Crosland

He was so depressed, he tried to commit suicide by inhaling
next to an Armenian.
Woody Allen

How about the raffle where the first prize was a week in
Belfast and the second prize was a fortnight in Belfast.
Brendan Behan

Australia is a country whose industrial and commercial development has been unspeakably retarded by an unfortunate dispute among geographers as to whether it is a continent or an island.

Ambrose Bierce

The ignorance of French society gives one a rough sense of the infinite.

Joseph Ernest Renan

The sun never sets on the British Empire because God wouldn't trust an Englishman in the dark.

Duncan Spaeth

The softer the currency in a foreign country, the harder the toilet paper.

John Fountain

The Irish climate is wonderful, but the weather ruins it.

Tony Butler

To be a Frenchman abroad is to be miserable; to be an American abroad is to make other people miserable.

Ambrose Bierce

We had a very successful trip to Russia – we got back.

Bob Hope

A gesticulation is any movement made by a foreigner.

J.B. Morton

I can never forgive God for creating the French.

Peter Ustinov

What do I think of Western civilisation? I think it would be a very good idea.

Mahatma Gandhi

When the missionaries came to Africa they had the Bible and we had the land. They said 'Let us pray.' We closed our eyes. When we opened them we had the Bible and they had the land.

Desmond Tutu

Nebraska is proof that hell is full and the dead walk the earth.

Liz Winston

Black Englishmen and women who win Olympic medals are described as English while those who riot and throw petrol bombs are invariably West Indian.

Edward Hughes

The English find ill-health not only interesting but respectable, and often experience death in the effort to avoid a fuss.

Pamela Frankau

It must be marvellous to be a man and just cheerfully assume I was superior. Better still, I could be an Irishman and have all the privileges of being male without giving up the right to be wayward, temperamental and an appealing minority.

Katharine Whitehorn

The English never smash in a face. They merely refrain from asking it to dinner.

Margaret Halsey

I have to choose between this world, the next world and Australia.

Oscar Wilde

Dutch is not so much a language as a disease of the throat

Mark Twain

In the Soviet Union a writer who is critical is taken to a lunatic asylum. In the United States, he is taken to a talk show.

Carlos Fuentes

When in Paris, I always eat at the Eiffel Tower restaurant because it's the only place where I can avoid seeing the damned thing.

William Morris

It is unthinkable for a Frenchman to arrive at middle age without having both syphilis and the Cross of the Legion of Honour.

André Gide

The US embassy in Moscow is nothing but an eight-storey microphone plugged into the Politburo.

Richard Armey

It is peculiar that all the sights in Rome are called after London cinemas.

Nancy Mitford

I never met anyone in Ireland who understood the Irish question, except one Englishman who had only been there a week.

Kenneth Fraser

One of the girls in my swimming squad complained that there were men in the women's changing room, only to discover on investigation that she had merely overheard East German girls in the next cubicle.

Charles Wilson

Going to the loo in a yacht in a French harbour is not so much goodbye as au revoir.

Noel Coward

An Iranian moderate is one who believes that the firing squad should be democratically elected.

Henry Kissinger

Nationalities and Places

When an Englishman is totally incapable of doing any work whatsoever, he describes himself on his income-tax form as a 'gentleman'.

Robert Lynd

I never believed in Santa Claus because I knew no white dude would come into a black neighbourhood after dark.

Dick Gregory

In January, the Americans announce a new invention. In February, the Russians announce they made the same discovery 20 years ago. In March, the Japanese start exporting the invention to the U.S.

Lloyd Cory

My rackets are run on strictly American lines and they're going to stay that way.

Al Capone

I went to Paris and stayed at the Hotel Demolition by Kirkpatrick.

Spike Milligan

There are three things to beware of: the hoof of a horse, the horn of a bull, and the smile of an Englishman.

Seumas MacManus

When asked his opinion of Welsh nationalism, Mr Thomas replied in three words, two of which were 'Welsh nationalism'.

Dylan Thomas

When I die I want to decompose in a barrel of porter and have it served in all the pubs in Dublin.

J.P. Donleavy

The great majority of Germans, realising the practical impos-sibility of speaking their own language with any degree of success, abandon it altogether and communicate with one another on brass bands.

Frank Richardson

I am not British. On the contrary.

Samuel Beckett

In Istanbul I was known as 'English Delight'.

Noel Coward

No bombardment of Rheims Cathedral can do anything like the damage that the last restoration did.

Roger Fry

The Great Wall, I've been told, is the only man-made structure on earth that is visible from the moon. For the life of me I cannot see why anyone would go to the moon to look at it, when, with almost the same difficulty, it can be viewed in China.

J.K. Galbraith

You gotta say this for the white race – its self-confidence knows no bounds. Who else could go to a small island in the South Pacific where there is no poverty, no crime, no unem-ployment, no war and no worry – and call it a 'primitive society'.

Dick Gregory

Americans are remorseless. They invite you to a party. You can't say 'I've got a splitting headache' – they'll send the doctor around.

V.S. Pritchett

American newspapers are too big, and their lavatory paper is too small.

Ernest Bevin

It is never difficult to distinguish between a Scotsman with a grievance and a ray of sunshine.

P.G. Wodehouse

Heaven is an English policeman, a French cook, a German engineer, an Italian lover and everything organised by the Swiss. Hell is an English cook, a French engineer, a German policeman, a Swiss lover and everything organised by the Italians.

John Elliot

America has become so tense and nervous, it's been years since I've seen anyone asleep in church.

Norman Vincent Peale

My ancestors were Puritans from England. They arrived in the United States in 1648 in the hope of finding greater restrictions than were permissible under English law at that time.

Garrison Keillor

I was in a library in Toronto in 1915, studying a Latin poet, and all of a sudden I thought, war can't be this bad. So I walked out and enlisted.

Lester B. Pearson

I was the toast of two continents – Greenland and Australia.

Dorothy Parker

In Italy for thirty years under the Borgias they had warfare, terror, murder, bloodshed, but they produced Michelangelo, Leonardo da Vinci, and the Renaissance. In Switzerland, they had brotherly love, they had five hundred years of democracy and peace. And what did they produce? The cuckoo-clock.

Orson Welles

The only time in his life that Joseph Joffre, French marshal, ever put up a fight was when asked for his resignation.

Winston Churchill

To live in Australia permanently is rather like going to a party and dancing all night with your mother.

Barry Humphries

Canada is a country so square that even the female impersonators are women.

Richard Brenner

The Welsh are the only nation in the world that has produced no graphic or plastic art, no architecture, no drama. They just sing. Sing and blow down instruments of plated silver.

Evelyn Waugh

New Zealand is a country of thirty thousand million sheep – three million of whom think they are human.

Barry Humphries

Sex is allowed in Scotland only when Rangers beat Celtic.

Ronnie Barker

Nationalities and Places

Cork, like Dublin, possesses a river, but there is no record that any Cork townsman has ever succeeded in spitting across it. This is not to say that the townsmen of Cork have given up trying. Indeed, some Cork townsmen endeavour to keep themselves in practice even when their beautiful river is not in sight.

Shamus O'Shamus

I once heard a Welsh sermon in which the word 'truth' was repeatedly uttered in English. Apparently there is no exact equivalent in Welsh.

Geoffrey Madan

In Ireland when the weather forecast is bad, it's invariably correct; when it's good, it's invariably wrong.

Tony Butler

The purpose of an introduction in England is to conceal the identities of two people from each other.

George Mikes

One Russian is an anarchist, two Russians are a chess game, three Russians are a revolution, and four Russians are the Budapest String Quartet.

Jascha Heifetz

If it was raining soup, the Irish would be out with forks.

Brendan Behan

Wales is the land of my fathers. And my fathers can have it.

Dylan Thomas

We can trace almost all the disasters of English history to the influence of Wales.

Evelyn Waugh

Nationalities and Places

The British tourist is always happy abroad as long as the natives are waiters.

Robert Morley

I like the English. They have the most rigid code of immorality in the world.

Malcolm Bradbury

Apart from cheese and tulips, the main product of Holland is advocaat, a drink made from lawyers.

Alan Coren

The United States, I believe, are under the impression that they are twenty years in advance of Britain; whilst, as a matter of actual verifiable fact, they are just about six hours behind it.

Harold Hobson

On the Continent, people have good food; in England people have good table manners.

George Mikes

I shook hands with a friendly Arab – I still have my right hand to prove it.

Spike Milligan

Life is too short to learn German.

Richard Porson

In India, a farm hand was caught in the act with his cow. He said he had bad eyesight and thought it was his wife.

Spike Milligan

They say that men become attached even to Widnes.

A.J. Taylor

Nationalities and Places

It is good to be on your guard against an Englishman who speaks French perfectly; he is likely to be a card sharp or an attaché in the diplomatic service.

Somerset Maugham

Homosexuality in Russia is a crime, and the punishment is seven years in prison, locked up with the other men. There is a three year waiting list.

Yakov Smirnoff

I had always imagined that cliché was a suburb of Paris, until I discovered it was a street in Oxford.

Philip Guedalla

On entering an English railway carriage it is customary to shake hands with all the passengers.

R. J. Phillips

Have you tried the famous echo in the Reading Room of the British Museum?

Gerard Hoffnung

Where but in Kenya can a man whose grandfather was a cannibal watch a really good game of polo?

Marina Sulzberger

The British may not be the greatest nation at winning Winter Olympics, but at least we can carry our bloody flag properly.

Mike Freeman

Names are not always what they seem. The common Welsh name BZJXXLLWCP is pronounced Jackson.

Mark Twain

Americans hardly ever retire from business; they are either carried out feet first or they jump from a window.

A.L. Goodheart

The devil will not come to Cornwall, for fear of being put into a pie.

Clement Freud

The Germans take part of a verb and put it down here, like a stake, and then they take the other part of it and put it over yonder like another stake, and between these two limits they just shovel in German.

Mark Twain

For some reason, a glaze passes over people's faces when you say Canada.

Sondra Gotlieb

The world still consists of two clearly divided groups; the English and the foreigners. One group consists of less than 50 million people; the other of 3,950 million. The latter group does not really count.

George Mikes

Students of Soviet affairs know how difficult it is to foretell the Soviet past.

George Paloczi-Horvath

The French have just invented a Michelin bomb – it destroys only restaurants with less than four stars.

Robin Williams

Russian comedians must be careful about what jokes they tell. If you say 'Take my wife, please,' when you get home, she's gone.

Yakov Smirnoff

As for marriage, it is one of America's most popular institutions. The American man marries early and the American woman marries often; and they get on extremely well together.

Oscar Wilde

193

A French Member of Parliament went to sleep for half an hour during a debate and when he woke he found he had been Prime Minister twice.

Oswald Lewis

Politics

Politics

The ideal form of government is democracy tempered with assassination.

Voltaire

Democracy is a pathetic belief in the collective wisdom of individual ignorance.

H.L. Mencken

I never trust a man unless I've got his pecker in my pocket.

Lyndon B. Johnson

Sure let him join our campaign. I'd prefer to have him inside our tent pissing out than outside our tent pissing in.

Lyndon B. Johnson

It is true that liberty is precious – so precious it must be carefully rationed.

V.I. Lenin

The cardinal rule of politics – never get caught in bed with a live man or a dead woman.

Larry Hagman

I do not belong to any organised political party – I am a Democrat.

Will Rogers

The main difference for the history of the world if I had been shot rather than Kennedy, is that Onassis probably wouldn't have married Mrs Khrushchev.

Nikita Khrushchev

It is now known that men enter local politics solely as a result of being unhappily married.

C.N. Parkinson

The Tories are nothing else but a load of kippers, two-faced with no guts.

Eric Heffer

The draft is white people sending black people to fight yellow people to protect the country they stole from red people.

James Rado

I never vote for anyone – I always vote against.

W.C. Fields

Watergate was the only brothel where the madam remained a virgin.

Mort Sahl

A fool and his money are soon elected.

Will Rogers

An honest politician is one who when he is bought, stays bought.

Simon Cameron

I don't make jokes. I just observe the government and report the facts.

Will Rogers

No comment, but don't quote me.

Dan Quayle

My family was in Irish politics while De Valera's was still bartering budgerigars on the back streets of Barcelona.

James Dillon

Politics

A statesman is a dead politician. We need more statesmen.

Bob Edwards

Stanley Baldwin is dead – the light in that great turnip has at last gone out.

Winston Churchill

A debate without the honourable member would be like Hamlet without the third grave digger.

Winston Churchill

Reader suppose you were an idiot; and suppose you were a member of Congress; but I repeat myself.

Mark Twain

I do not see the EEC as a great love affair. It is more like nine middle-aged couples with failing marriages meeting at a Brussels hotel for a group grope.

Kenneth Tynan

The government has been faced with an orchestrated campaign of pressure by the newspapers. They even had the gargantuan intellect of Bernard Levin squeaking away in the undergrowth like a demented vole.

Denis Healey

If you don't say anything you won't be called on to repeat it.

Calvin Coolidge

One of the things that being in politics has taught me is that men are not a reasoned or a reasonable sex.

Margaret Thatcher

Politics

Sir Robert Peel's smile is like the silver fittings on a coffin. The Right Honourable Gentleman is reminiscent of a poker. The only difference is that a poker gives off occasional signs of warmth.

Benjamin Disraeli

The difference between a misfortune and a calamity is this: if Gladstone fell into the Thames, it would be a misfortune. But if someone dragged him out again, that would be a calamity.

Benjamin Disraeli

All political parties die at last of swallowing their own lies.

John Arbuthnot

I'm glad I'm not Brezhnev. Being the Russian leader in the Kremlin, you never know if someone's tape-recording what you say.

Richard M. Nixon

Richard Nixon told us he was going to take crime off the streets. He did. He took it into the White House.

Ralph Abernathy

The speeches of Warren Harding left the impression of an army of pompous phrases moving over the landscape in search of an idea. Sometimes these meandering words would actually capture a straggling thought and bear it triumphantly a prisoner in their midst, until it died of servitude and overwork.

William McAdoo

During Stalin's speeches to the Praesidium, the first delegate to stop clapping was routinely hauled off to be shot.

Clive James

Politics

The purpose of the Presidential Office is not power, or leadership of the Western World, but reminiscence, bestselling reminiscence.

Roger Jellinek

Sometimes I look at Billy and Jimmy and I say to myself 'Lillian, you should have stayed a virgin.'

Lillian Carter

Actually, I vote Labour – but my butler's Tory.

Louis Mountbatten

Chamberlain seemed such a nice old gentleman that I thought I would give him my autograph.

Adolf Hitler

He has all the characteristics of a dog except loyalty.

Sam Houston

You'll notice that Nancy Reagan never drinks water when Ronnie speaks.

Robin Williams

Some Republicans are so ignorant they wouldn't know how to pour piss out of a boot – even if the instructions were printed on the heel.

Lyndon B. Johnson

When the President does it, that means it's not illegal.

Richard M. Nixon

Tony Benn is the Bertie Wooster of Marxism.

Malcolm Bradbury

Gerald Ford looks like the guy in a science fiction movie who is first to see the Creature.

David Frye

Politics

The Vice-Presidency isn't worth a pitcher of warm spit.

J.N. Garner

A politician is any citizen with influence enough to get his old mother a job as a charwoman in the City Hall.

H.L. Mencken

It's easy being a humorist when you've got the whole government working for you.

Will Rogers

I like Republicans, and I would trust them with anything in the world except public office.

Adlai Stevenson

I am sorry that I cannot address the people of Latin America in their own language which is Latin.

Dan Quayle

Stanley Baldwin occasionally stumbled over the truth, but hastily picked himself up and hurried on as if nothing had happened.

Winston Churchill

Richard Nixon is a no-good, lying bastard. He can lie out of both sides of his mouth at the same time, and if he ever caught himself telling the truth, he'd lie just to keep his hand in.

Harry S. Truman

An aristocracy in a republic is like a chicken whose head has been cut off: it may run about in a lively way, but in fact it is dead.

Nancy Mitford

He who throws mud loses ground.

Adlai Stevenson

When you say that you agree to a thing in principle you mean that you have not the slightest intention of carrying it out in practice.

Otto von Bismarck

Chamberlain has the mind and manner of a clothes-brush.

Harold Nicholson

Ronald Reagan has done for monetarism what the Boston Strangler did for door-to-door salesmen.

Denis Healey

A committee is a group of people who individually can do nothing, but together decide that nothing can be done.

Fred Allen

Richard Needham is a man who, having escaped from the *Titanic*, has clambered aboard the *Marie Celeste*.

Peter Sharpe

Arthur Scargill couldn't negotiate his way out of a toilet.

Ray Lynk

The Liberals are Dr Barnado's home for orphan voters.

Gerry Neale

Paul Channon is educated beyond his intelligence.

Dennis Skinner

The Social Democrats are the heterosexual wing of the Liberal Party.

George Foulkes

An ambassador is a person who, having failed to secure an office from the people, is given one by the Administration on condition that he leave the country.

Ambrose Bierce

I have no interest in sailing round the world. Not that there is any lack of requests for me to do so.

Edward Heath

A philosopher Tory, like military intelligence, is a contradiction in terms.

Michael Foot

The right honourable gentleman is indebted to his memory for his jests, and to his imagination for his facts.

Richard Brinsley Sheridan

I never drink coffee at lunch – I find it keeps me awake for the afternoon.

Ronald Reagan

The government solution to any problem is usually at least as bad as the problem.

Milton Friedman

To err is Truman.

Walter Winchell

A committee is a group of the unwilling, picked from the unfit, to do the unnecessary.

Richard Harkness

All animals are equal but some are more equal than others.

George Orwell

Apart from that Mrs Lincoln, how did you enjoy the play?

Tom Lehrer

Given half a chance, politicians would give lower taxes and extra social security concessions to marginal constituencies only.

William Keegan

Politics

William Whitelaw is one of the last representatives of a dying Tory tradition – possession of land, enthusiasm for shooting small birds, and antipathy for reading books.

Roy Hattersley

Politics is the art of choosing between the disastrous and the unpalatable.

John K. Galbraith

Neil Kinnock looks like a tortoise having an orgasm.

Patrick Murray

I wouldn't believe that Hitler was dead, even if he told me himself.

Hjalmar Schacht

Clement Attlee reminds me of nothing so much as a dead fish before it has had time to stiffen.

George Orwell

The Labour Party's election manifesto is the longest suicide note in history.

Greg Knight

I don't know what I would do without Whitelaw. Everyone should have a Willy.

Margaret Thatcher

I always have one golden rule for such occasions – I ask myself what Nanny would have expected me to do.

Lord Carrington

Put three Zionists in a room – and they will form four political parties.

Levi Eshkol

Now and then an innocent man is elected to the legislature.

Frank McKinney

I met Lord Curzon in Downing Street and received from him the sort of greeting a corpse would give to an undertaker.

Stanley Baldwin

I want it so that you can't wipe your ass on a piece of paper that hasn't got my picture on it.

Lyndon B. Johnson

Neville Chamberlain might make an adequate Lord Mayor of Birmingham – in a lean year.

David Lloyd George

The function of socialism is to raise suffering to a higher level.

Norman Mailer

Revolution is a trivial shift in the emphasis of suffering.

Tom Stoppard

Winston Churchill would kill his own mother just so that he could use her skin to make a drum to beat his own praises.

Margot Asquith

When more and more people are thrown out of work unemployment results.

Calvin Coolidge

Politics is the art of looking for trouble, finding it everywhere, diagnosing it wrongly and applying unsuitable remedies.

Ernest Benn

I don't know what people have got against the government – they've done nothing.

Bob Hope

An infallible method of conciliating a tiger is to allow oneself to be devoured.

Konrad Adenauer

McKinley has about as much backbone as a chocolate eclair.

Theodore Roosevelt

The illegal we do immediately. The unconstitutional takes a little longer.

Henry Kissinger

Politicians are wedded to the truth, but like many other married couples they sometimes live apart.

H.H. Munro

De Valera discloses the workings of a mind to which incoherence lends an illusion of profundity.

T. de Vere-White

Ted Heath is a politician past his sell by date.

Neil Kinnock

Get all the fools on your side and you can be elected to anything.

Frank Dane

I haven't heard from our ambassador to Spain in three years. If he doesn't contact me in the next year, I intend to write.

George Washington

A typical speech by Margaret Thatcher sounds like the Book of Revelations read over a railway station public address system by a headmistress of a certain age wearing calico knickers.

Clive James

Robert Muldoon is a bull who carries his own china shop with him.

Inder Jit

The voters have spoken – the bastards.

Richard M. Nixon

Winston Churchill never spares himself in conversation. He gives himself so generously that hardly anybody else is permitted to give anything in his presence.

Aneurin Bevan

Intervening in Gerald Ford's re-election campaign is like re-arranging the deck chairs on the *Titanic*.

Rogers Morton

Harold Wilson is going around the country stirring up apathy.

William Whitelaw

He stood twice for Parliament, but so diffidently that his candidature passed almost unnoticed.

Evelyn Waugh

If you would know the depth and meanness of human nature, you have got to be a prime minister running a general election.

John A. MacDonald

I always wanted to get into politics, but I was never light enough to make the team.

Art Buchwald

If you walk like a duck, and you quack like a duck, and you say you're a duck, you are a duck.

George Bush

Ninety per cent of the politicians give the other ten per cent a bad reputation.

Henry Kissinger

I have reason to believe that the fowl pest outbreaks are the work of the IRA.

Ian Paisley

Walter Mondale has all the charisma of a speed bump.

Will Durst

So Reagan consults an astrologer – I'm glad he consults somebody.

Jim Wright

I have always found F.D. Roosevelt an amusing fellow, but I would not employ him, except for reasons of personal friendship, as a geek in a common carnival.

Murray Kempton

I am extraordinarily patient, provided I get my own way in the end.

Margaret Thatcher

George Washington was ignorant of the commonest accomplishments of youth. He could not even lie.

Mark Twain

A year ago Gerald Ford was unknown throughout America. Now he's unknown throughout the world.

Norman Mailer

The supporters I value are those who will support me when I am wrong. Anyone can support me when I am right.

W.L. Melbourne

I have orders to be awakened at any time in case of a national emergency, even if I'm in a cabinet meeting.

Ronald Reagan

There are only three men who have ever understood the Schleswig-Holstein question. One was Prince Albert, who is dead. The second was a German professor, who became mad. I am the third and I have forgotten all about it.

Viscount Palmerston

Mr Lloyd George spoke for a hundred and seventeen minutes, in which period he was detected only once in the use of an argument.

Arnold Bennett

I have not met Norman Scott face to face for many years.

Jeremy Thorpe

He may be a son of a bitch, but at least he's our son of a bitch.

Franklin Roosevelt

Who is King Billy? Go home man and read your Bible.

Ian Paisley

One could drive a prairie schooner through any part of the arguments of William Jennings Bryan and never scrape against a fact.

David Huston

I have only two regrets – that I have not shot Henry Clay or hanged John C. Calhoun.

Andrew Jackson

Charles De Gaulle looked like a female llama surprised in her bath.

Winston Churchill

Republicans sleep in twin beds, some even in separate rooms. That's why there are more Democrats.

Walt Stanton

As for the look on Dan Quayle's face – how to describe it? If a tree fell in a forest, and no one was there to hear it, it might sound like Dan Quayle looks.

Tom Shales

Stanley Baldwin – one could not even dignify him with the name of stuffed shirt. He was simply a hole in the air.

George Orwell

The Secret Service is under orders that if Bush is shot, to shoot Quayle.

John Kerry

If the word 'No' was removed from the English language, Ian Paisley would be speechless.

John Hume

If Nixon's secretary, Rosemary Woods, had been Moses' secretary, there would only have been eight commandments.

Art Buchwald

Ninety-nine per cent of the adults in this country are decent, hard-working, honest Americans. It's the other lousy one per cent that gets all the publicity and gives us a bad name. But then, we elected them.

Lily Tomlin

Nixon impeached himself. He gave us Gerald Ford as revenge.

Bella Abzug

The more you read about politics, the more you have got to admit that each party is worse than the other.

Will Rogers

The League of Nations is like sheep passing resolutions in favour of vegetarianism.

Dean Inge

At every crisis the Kaiser crumpled. In defeat, he fled; in revolution he abdicated; in exile he remarried.

Winston Churchill

The House of Lords is a model of how to care for the elderly.

Frank Field

For socialists, going to bed with the Liberals is like having oral sex with a shark.

Larry Zolf

I am thoroughly in favour of Mrs Thatcher's visit to the Falk-lands. I find a bit of hesitation, though, about her coming back.

John Mortimer

Communism is the lay form of Catholicism.

George Bernard Shaw

The British Labour Party is more Methodist than Marxist.

Morgan Phillips

The US communist party was at one stage so heavily infiltrated by FBI undercover agents that they outnumbered the actual communists.

Louis Heren

Keith Joseph is a mixture of Rasputin and Tommy Cooper.

Denis Healey

There cannot be a world crisis next week, my schedule is full.

Henry Kissinger

 **Politics**

My one ardent desire is that after the war Lloyd George
should be publicly castrated in front of Edith Cavell's statue.
Lytton Strachey

The British Secret Service was staffed at one period almost
entirely by alcoholic homosexuals working for the KGB.
Clive James

I know I'm getting better at golf because I'm hitting fewer
spectators.
Gerald R. Ford

Everywhere in England and America statesmen were already
preparing their triumphs of 1914 and 1939, by spending
long days on the golf course and long nights at the bridge
table.
Osbert Sitwell

Have you ever noticed how England wins the World Cup
only under a Labour government?
Harold Wilson

There is a man standing at the bottom of Niagara Falls trying
to push the water back with his hands. He is Public
Relations Officer to the Prime Minister and the Cabinet.
William Connor

The Labour Party have lost the last four elections. If they
lose another, they get to keep the Liberal Party.
Clive Anderson

Stafford Cripps has a first rate mind until he makes it up.
Violet Asquith

Richard Nixon was offered $2 million by Schick to do a
television commercial for Gillette.
Gerald R. Ford

When they circumcised Herbert Samuel, they threw away the wrong bit.

David Lloyd George

A committee is a cul-de-sac into which ideas are lured and then quietly strangled.

Barnett Cocks

Ronald Reagan is a triumph of the embalmer's art.

Gore Vidal

They think that whenever anyone in the White House now tells a lie I get a royalty.

Richard M. Nixon

Ronald Reagan won because he ran against Jimmy Carter. If he had run unopposed he would have lost.

Mort Sahl

I am still heavyweight champion of Uganda. Nobody is willing to fight me.

Idi Amin

President Calvin Coolidge was the greatest man ever came out of Plymouth Corner, Vermont.

Clarence Darrow

How was I to know that the B-1 was an airplane? I thought it was vitamins for the troops.

Ronald Reagan

The truth is that men are tired of liberty.

Benito Mussolini

Religion

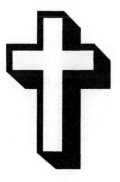

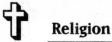

Not only is there no God, but try getting a plumber at weekends.

Woody Allen

God made everything out of nothing. But the nothingness shows through.

Paul Valéry

The men who really believe in themselves are all in lunatic asylums.

G.K. Chesterton

A good sermon should be like a woman's skirt: short enough to rouse the interest, but long enough to cover the essentials.

Ronald Knox

Peter remained on friendly terms with Christ even though Christ had healed his mother-in-law.

Samuel Butler

How can I believe in God when only last week I got my tongue caught in the roller of an electric typewriter?

Woody Allen

The trouble with most of us is that we have been inoculated with small doses of Christianity in childhood which keeps us from catching the real thing.

Bob Phillips

He was of the faith chiefly in the sense that the church he currently did not attend was Catholic.

Kingsley Amis

I don't believe in astrology because I'm a Gemini, and Geminis never believe in astrology.

Raymond Smullyan

Millions long for immortality who do not know what to do with themselves on a rainy Sunday afternoon.

Susan Ertz

Woman was God's second mistake.

Friedrich Nietzsche

As God once said, and I think rightly ...

Margaret Thatcher

I'm astounded by people who want to 'know' the universe when it's so hard to find your way around Chinatown.

Woody Allen

I do benefits for all religions – I'd hate to blow the hereafter on a technicality.

Bob Hope

Some people say there is a God; others say there is no God. The truth probably lies somewhere in between.

W.B. Yeats

Philosophy is unintelligible answers to insoluble problems.

Henry B. Adams

I have spent a lot of time searching through the Bible for loopholes.

W.C. Fields

The Bible tells us to love our neighbours, and also to love our enemies; probably because they are generally the same people.

G.K. Chesterton

I'm really a timid person – I was beaten up by Quakers.

Woody Allen

Sir, a woman preaching is like a dog walking on its hind legs.
You don't expect it to be done well – you are surprised to
find it done at all.

Samuel Johnson

An atheist is a guy who watches a Notre Dame versus SMU
football game and doesn't care who wins.

Dwight D. Eisenhower

On the question of eternal punishment, the word 'eternal'
did not appear to the elders of St Osoph's to designate a
sufficiently long period of time.

Stephen Leacock

Hearing nuns' confessions is like being stoned to death with
popcorn.

Fulton J. Sheen

I have tried in my time to be a philosopher, but cheerfulness
always kept breaking in.

Oliver Edwards

The word *good* has many meanings. For example, if a man
were to shoot his grandmother at a range of five hundred
yards, I should call him a good shot, but not necessarily a
good man.

G.K. Chesterton

Thank God I'm an atheist.

Luis Buñuel

The Bible was a consolation to a fellow alone in the old cell.
The lovely thin paper with a bit of mattress stuffing in it, if
you could get a match, was as good a smoke as ever I tasted.

Brendan Behan

Become a Protestant? Certainly not. Just because I've lost my faith doesn't mean I've lost my reason.

James Joyce

If you want to make God laugh, tell him your future plans.

Woody Allen

Why do born again people so often make you wish they had never been born the first time?

Katharine Whitehorn

I do not believe in an after life, although I am bringing a change of underwear.

Woody Allen

The Anglo-Saxon conscience doesn't stop you from sinning; it just stops you from enjoying it.

Salvador de Madariaga

How was I to know that the Pope was a Catholic? Nobody's infallible.

George Brown

Only one man ever understood me – and he didn't understand me.

G. W. Hegel

They say that Joseph Smith did not receive from the hands of an angel the written revelation that we obey. Let them prove it!

Brigham Young

I desire to go to hell and not to heaven. In the former place I shall enjoy the company of Popes, Kings and Princes, while in the latter are only beggars, monks and apostles.

Niccolo Machiavelli

An archbishop is an ecclesiastical dignitary one point holier than a bishop.

Ambrose Bierce

He is such a devout Catholic, he won't be happy until he is crucified.

John B. Keane

One of the crying needs of the time is for a suitable Burial Service for the admittedly damned.

H.L. Mencken

Life is the ever dwindling period between abortion and euthanasia.

Patrick Murray

I haven't been to Mass for years. I've got every mortal sin on my conscience, but I know when I'm doing wrong. I'm still a Catholic.

Angus Wilson

The sewing-circle is the Protestant confessional, where each one confesses, not her own sins, but the sins of her neighbours.

Charles B. Fairbanks

When I was a kid, I used to pray every night for a new bicycle. Then I realised that the Lord doesn't work that way, so I just stole one and asked Him to forgive me.

Emo Philips

I'm a communist by day and a Catholic after it gets dark.

Brendan Behan

Few sinners are saved after the first twenty minutes of a sermon.

Mark Twain

Monica Baldwin's book *I Leapt over the Wall* strengthened my desire not to become a nun.

Noel Coward

Malcolm Muggeridge was a thief crucified between two Christs.

Anthony Powell

Plenty well, no pray. Big bellyache, heap God.

Geronimo

The secret of a good sermon is to have a good beginning and a good ending and having the two as close together as possible.

George Burns

Things have come to a pretty pass when religion is allowed to invade the sphere of private life.

W.L. Melbourne

I would have made a good Pope.

Richard M. Nixon

Where would Christianity be if Jesus had got eight to fifteen years with time off for good behaviour?

James Donovan

I expect you know my friend Evelyn Waugh, who, like you, your Holiness is a Roman Catholic.

Randolph Churchill

There is a species of person called a 'Modern Churchman' who draws the full salary of a beneficed clergyman and need not commit himself to any religious belief.

Evelyn Waugh

I know I am God because when I pray to him I find I'm talking to myself.

Peter Barnes

I never quite forgave Mahaffy for getting himself suspended from preaching in the College Chapel. Ever since his sermons were discontinued, I suffer from insomnia in church.

George Tyrrell

Would you, my dear young friends, like to be inside with the five wise virgins, or outside, alone and in the dark with the five foolish ones?

Montagu Butler

I never heard him cursing; I don't believe he was ever drunk in his life – sure he's not like a Christian at all.

Sean O'Casey

I was brought up in a clergyman's household, so I am a first-class liar.

Sybil Thorndyke

It is a sin to believe in the evil of others, but it is seldom a mistake.

H.L. Mencken

My ancestors wandered lost in the wilderness for forty years because even in biblical times men would not stop to ask for directions.

Elayne Boosler

God is love, but get it in writing.

Gypsy Rose Lee

I was raised in the Jewish tradition, taught never to marry a Gentile woman, shave on a Saturday night and, most especially, never to shave a Gentile woman on a Saturday night.

Woody Allen

Maybe this world is another planet's hell.

Aldous Huxley

When we talk to God, we're praying. When God talks to us we're schizophrenic.

Lily Tomlin

Eternal torment is almost certain for the vast majority: but a very few may hope for merciful annihilation.

Hugh Cecil

The *Revised Prayer Book* is an attempt to suppress burglary by legalising petty larceny.

Dean Inge

Lies are defensible in the face of an attempt to extract personal information by direct question.

John Henry Newman

There is a lost Scottish community, long unable to read or write. They preserve one relic only of Protestantism, that if they get hold of any meat, they keep it until Friday to eat.

G.M. Young

The Commandments don't tell you what you ought to do: they only put ideas into your head.

Elizabeth Bibesco

Perhaps the most lasting pleasure in life is the pleasure of not going to church.

Dean Inge

Jesus was born on a bank holiday and died on a bank holiday. We can therefore assume that when he returns again it will also be on a bank holiday.

P. G. Johnson

I don't pray because I don't want to bore God.

Orson Welles

✝ Religion

I must believe in the Apostolic Succession, there being no other way of accounting for the descent of the Bishop of Exeter from Judas Iscariot.

Sydney Smith

A church is a place in which clergymen who have never been to heaven preach about it to people who will never get there.

H.L. Mencken

There are three sexes – men, women and clergymen.

Sydney Smith

The three great elements of modern civilisation were gunpowder, printing, and the Protestant Religion.

Thomas Carlyle

Sleep is good, death is better; but the best thing would be never to have been born at all.

Heinrich Heine

How could God do this to me after all I've done for him?

King Louis XIV

When a woman gets too old to be attractive to man, she turns to God.

Honoré de Balzac

I once heard of a prophet who, when he baptised converts, at night, in a deep river, also drowned them, so that, being cleansed of sin and having no time to sin again, they went straight to Paradise.

Joyce Cary

I have noticed again and again since I have been in the church that lay interest in ecclesiastical matters is often a prelude to insanity.

Evelyn Waugh

Moss Hart's elegant country house and grounds are just what God would have done if He had the money.

Alexander Woollcott

Vouchsafe O Lord, to keep us this day without being found out.

Samuel Butler

Mr Kremlin himself was distinguished for his ignorance, for he had only one idea and that was wrong.

Benjamin Disraeli

All are lunatics, but he who can analyse his delusions is called a philosopher.

Ambrose Bierce

If you want to make a man very angry, tell him you are going to pray for him.

Edgar W. Howe

I'm Jewish. I don't work out. If God had wanted us to bend over, He would have put diamonds on the floor.

Joan Rivers

There is not the least use in preaching to anyone unless you chance to catch them ill.

Sydney Smith

I am increasingly convinced that the *Church Times* is now edited by the Devil in person.

Bishop Gore

The principal reason for the increase in the number of misprints in literature is the increasingly liberal attitude of the Church of England. Not enough parsons are unfrocked these days. The unfortunates of earlier days were often happy to find themselves employment in printing houses, correcting proofs.

David Holloway

'Meet my daughter', said the bishop, with some disgust.
Evelyn Waugh

'Take my camel, dear,' said my Aunt Dot, as she climbed
down from this animal on her return from High Mass.
Rose Macaulay

A dead atheist is someone who's all dressed up with nowhere
to go.
James Duffecy

A Calvinistic Presbyterian believes that all Catholics will be
damned because they are predestined to be damned; an
ordinary Presbyterian believes that all Catholics will be
damned on their merits.
John Bartley

What do people say when God sneezes?
Henny Youngman

I'm not Jewish – it's just that a tree fell on me.
Spike Milligan

Give me a no-nonsense down to earth behaviourist, a few
drugs and simple electrical appliances, and in six months I
will have him reciting the Athaniasian creed in public.
W.H. Auden

God can stand being told by Professor Ayer and Margharita
Laski that He does not exist.
J.B. Priestley

The Bible tells us to forgive our enemies; not our friends.
Margot Asquith

Religion

The most scandalous charges against the Pope were suppressed. His Holiness was accused only of piracy, rape, murder, sodomy and incest.

Edward Gibbon

My dear child, you must believe in God in spite of what the clergy tell you.

Margot Asquith

What he lacked in depth as a preacher he made up for in length.

Mark Twain

Science and Technology

Ouch!

Isaac Newton

In ancient times they had no statistics so they had to fall back on lies.

Stephen Leacock

The speed at which boiling milk rises from the bottom of the pan to any point beyond the top is greater than the speed at which the human brain and hand can combine to snatch the confounded thing off.

H.F. Ellis

Statistics are like loose women; once you get your hands on them you can do anything you like with them.

Walt Michaels

An expert is someone who has made all the mistakes that can be made, but in a very narrow field.

Niels Bohr

Everybody talks about the weather, but nobody does anything about it.

Charles D. Warner

It is impossible to combine the heating of milk with any other pursuit whatever.

H.F. Ellis

How does the little busy bee improve each shining hour and gather honey all the day from every opening flower? Well, he does not. He spends most of the day in buzzing and aimless acrobatics, and gets about a fifth of the honey he would collect if he organised himself.

Heneage Ogilvie

He uses statistics as a drunken man uses a lamp post – more for support than illumination.

Andrew Lang

To pray is to ask that the laws of the universe be annulled on behalf of a single petitioner confessedly unworthy.

Ambrose Bierce

Descended from the apes? Let us hope that is not true. But if it is, let us pray that it may not become generally known.

F.A. Montagu

Living on Earth may be expensive, but it includes an annual free trip around the sun.

Ashleigh Brilliant

Ketchup left overnight on dinner plates has a longer half-life than radioactive waste.

Wes Smith

How do they get that non-stick stuff to stick to the frying pan?

Steven Wright

Why don't they make the whole plane out of that black box stuff?

Steven Wright

Computer dating is fine – if you're a computer.

Rita May Brown

You can have a Model T Ford car any colour you like, so long as it's black.

Henry Ford

Get your facts right first and then you can distort them as much as you please.

Mark Twain

Science and Technology

Smoking is one of the leading causes of statistics.

Fletcher Knebel

There are lies, damn lies, and statistics.

Mark Twain

Outer space is no place for a person of breeding.

Violet Bonham Carter

I put some instant coffee in the microwave oven the other night and I got a time reversal.

Steven Wright

We've got to take the atom bomb seriously – it's dynamite.

Samuel Goldwyn

The guy who invented the first wheel was an idiot, but the guy who invented the other three, now he was a genius.

Sid Caesar

I bought some batteries, but they weren't included.

Steven Wright

The scientific theory I like best is that the rings of Saturn are composed entirely of lost airline luggage.

Mark Russell

If there had been a computer in 1872 it would have predicted that by now there would be so many horse-drawn vehicles that the entire surface of the earth would be ten feet deep in horse manure.

Karl Kapp

Biologically speaking, if something bites you, it is more likely to be female.

Desmond Morris

Science and Technology

I knew immediately when I had reached the North Pole, because in one step the north wind became a south wind.
Robert Peary

He was a good citizen, an upright man, and an ardent patriot, but of limited information regarding circular saws.
Stephen Leacock

Computers are improving – perhaps even to the point of writing poetry as good as that composed by a drunken poet.
Louis T. Milic

Asking an aerospace worker if he's ever been laid off before is like asking a mother if she's ever had a baby.
Richard Kapusta

Anybody who says he's been eaten by a wolf is a liar.
J.B. Theberge

All sorts of computer errors are now turning up. You'd be surprised to know the number of doctors who claim they are treating pregnant men.
Isaac Asimov

Damn the Solar System. Bad light; planets too distant, pestered with comets; feeble contrivance; could make better myself.
Francis Jeffery

Hell must be isothermal, for otherwise the resident engineers and physical chemists (of whom there must be many) could set up a heat engine to run a refrigerator to cool off a portion of their surroundings to any desired temperature.
Henry A. Bent

To err is human, but to really foul things up you need a computer.
Paul Ehrlich

Science and Technology

When I die, I'm going to leave my body to science fiction.

Steven Wright

I have a seashell collection; maybe you've seen it? I keep it on beaches all over the world.

Steven Wright

The most useful and least expensive household repair tool is the telephone.

Wes Smith

When you've seen one Redwood, you've seen 'em all.

Ronald Reagan

Science has conquered many diseases, broken the genetic code and even placed human beings on the moon, yet when a man of eighty is left in a room with two eighteen-year-old cocktail waitresses, nothing happens. Because the real problems never change.

Woody Allen

Inanimate objects can be classified scientifically into three major categories - those that don't work, those that break down and those that get lost.

Russell Baker

I have just invented an anti-gravity machine. It's called a chair.

Richard Feynman

Social Behaviour and Manners

In my experience, if you have to keep the lavatory door shut by extending your left leg, it's modern architecture.

Nancy Banks-Smith

The general advertiser's attitude would seem to be: if you are a lousy, smelly, idle, under-privileged, overweight and over-sexed status-seeking neurotic moron, give me your money.

Kenneth Bromfield

Style is when they're running you out of town and you make it look like you're leading a parade.

William Battie

An acquaintance is someone we know well enough to borrow from but not well enough to lend to.

Ambrose Bierce

There are many who dare not kill themselves for fear of what the neighbours will say.

Cyril Connolly

As far as I'm concerned there are only two kinds of people in the world – those who are kind to their servants and those who are not.

Duke of Argyll

I told the traffic warden to go forth and multiply, though not exactly in those words.

Woody Allen

As yet, Bernard Shaw hasn't become prominent enough to have any enemies; but none of his friends like him.

Oscar Wilde

There is only one immutable law in life – in a gentleman's toilet, incoming traffic has the right of way.

Hugh Leonard

It is illegal to make liquor privately or water publicly.

Lord Birkett

Know him? I know him so well that I haven't spoken to him for ten years.

Oscar Wilde

The full potentialities of human fury cannot be reached until a friend of both parties tactfully intervenes.

G.K. Chesterton

He was a great patriot, a humanitarian, a loyal friend – provided of course he really is dead.

Voltaire

Don't touch a woman's knee at the dinner table; she has an instinctive knowledge whether a man who touches her knee is caressing her or only wiping his greasy fingers on her stocking.

George Moore

Always forgive your enemies. Nothing annoys them so much.

Oscar Wilde

The only thing I really mind about going to prison is the thought of Lord Longford coming to visit me.

Richard Ingrams

Whatever you have read I have said is almost certainly untrue, except if it is funny in which case I *definitely* said it.

Tallulah Bankhead

If any reader of this book is in the grip of some habit of which he is deeply ashamed, I advise him not to give way to it in secret but to do it on television. No one will pass him with averted gaze on the other side of the street. People will cross the road at the risk of losing their own lives in order to say 'We saw you on the telly.'

Denis Pratt

I once sent a dozen of my friends a telegram saying FLEE AT ONCE – ALL IS DISCOVERED.
They all left town immediately.

Mark Twain

Anyone can do any amount of work provided it isn't the work he is supposed to be doing at the moment.

Robert Benchley

A pessimist is a man who, when he smells flowers, looks around for the coffin.

H.L. Mencken

When you have to kill a man it costs nothing to be polite.

Winston Churchill

I am free of all prejudice. I hate everyone equally.

W.C. Fields

When little men cast long shadows, the sun is about to set.

Michael Seymour

There is nothing like the sight of an old enemy down on his luck.

Euripides

If you cannot say anything good about someone, sit right here by me.

Alice Roosevelt

Those who give up smoking aren't the heroes. The real heroes are the rest of us – who have to listen to them.

Hal Boyle

I do not have to forgive my enemies – I have had them all shot.

Ramon Narvaez

Wit is like caviar. It should be served in small elegant portions and not splashed about like marmalade.

Noel Coward

One should never be unnecessarily rude to a lady except in street cars.

O. Henry

Blown his brains out you say? He must have been an incredibly good shot.

Noel Coward

I have a most peaceable disposition. My desires are for a modest hut, a thatched roof, a good bed, good food, very fresh milk and butter, flowers in front of my window and a few pretty trees by my door. And should the good Lord wish to make me really happy, he will allow me the pleasure of seeing about six or seven of my enemies hanged upon those trees.

Heinrich Heine

I regret very much my inability to attend your banquet. It is the baby's night out and I must stay at home with the nurse.

Ring Lardner

If this is the way that Queen Victoria treats her prisoners, she doesn't deserve to have any.

Oscar Wilde

It is perfectly monstrous the way people go about nowadays saying things against one, behind one's back, that are absolutely and entirely true.

Oscar Wilde

The louder he talked of his honour, the faster we counted our spoons.

R. W. Emerson

It is well known that if you stop and wind the window down to ask someone the way, he invariably turns out to be either deaf, senile, or a stranger there himself.

Lambert Jeffries

People often say to me 'What are you doing in my garden?'
Michael Redmond

Never murder a man when he's busy committing suicide.
Woodrow Wilson

If only these old walls could talk, how boring they would be.
Robert Benchley

I must decline your invitation owing to an engagement I am just about to make.

Oscar Wilde

The easiest way to give up smoking is to stop putting cigarettes in your mouth and lighting them.
William Rushton

I always pass on good advice – it's the only thing one can do with it.

Oscar Wilde

From the silence that prevails I conclude that Lauderdale has been telling a joke.

Richard Brinsley Sheridan

First left, go along the corridor. You'll see a door marked Gentlemen, but don't let that deter you.

F.E. Smith

It is very easy to endure the difficulties of one's enemies. It is the successes of one's friends that are hard to bear.

Oscar Wilde

The cocktail party – as the name itself indicates – was originally invented by dogs. They are simply bottom-sniffings raised to the rank of formal ceremonies.

Lawrence Durrell

This year Elizabeth Taylor is wearing Orson Welles designer jeans.

Joan Rivers

Frank Harris has been invited to every great house in England – once.

Oscar Wilde

Here's a rule I recommend. Never practise two vices at once.

Tallulah Bankhead

I can resist everything except temptation.

Oscar Wilde

There is not a single person between the ages of fifteen and twenty-five in the whole of Bicester or Welwyn Garden City who does not have to be woken every morning with stimulants in order that he may drift through the day on sedatives.

Quentin Crisp

Fashion is a form of ugliness so intolerable that we have to alter it every six months.

Oscar Wilde

I've had a wonderful evening – but this wasn't it.

Groucho Marx

You should study the Peerage; it is the best thing in fiction the English have ever done.

Oscar Wilde

I live in terror of not being misunderstood.

Oscar Wilde

If you can keep your head when all about you are losing theirs, it is possible you haven't grasped the gravity of the situation.

Jean Kerr

A careful driver is one who looks in both directions when he passes a red light.

Ralph Marterie

The extraordinary thing about the lower classes in England is that they are always losing their relations. They are extremely fortunate in that respect.

Oscar Wilde

Fate bestowed on M. Genet certain special advantages. He was illegitimate and spent his childhood in an orphanage. From there he graduated to a reformatory.

Quentin Crisp

If you don't go to other men's funerals, they won't go to yours.

Clarence S. Day

Giving up smoking is the easiest thing in the world. I know because I've done it thousands of times.

Mark Twain

Whoever thinks of going to bed before twelve o'clock is a scoundrel.

Samuel Johnson

Don't forget to tell everyone it's a secret.

Gerald F. Lieberman

I don't care to belong to any club that will accept me as a member.

Groucho Marx

I have often envied Gerry Wellesley the faculty of giving people rapid and often accurate information.

Harold Nicolson

The English country gentleman galloping after a fox – the unspeakable in full pursuit of the uneatable.

Oscar Wilde

Every normal man must be tempted, at times, to spit on his hands, hoist the black flag, and begin slitting throats.

H.L. Mencken

I'd rather eat shit than wear a suit.

Billy Carter

Some people can stay longer in an hour than others can in a week.

William D. Howells

Never rub bottoms with a porcupine.

Jane Philbin

Never in the history of fashion has so little material been raised so high to reveal so much that needs to be covered so badly.

Cecil Beaton

All the things I really like are either immoral, illegal or fattening.

Alexander Woollcott

The perfect hostess will see to it that books written by male and female authors be properly separated on her bookshelves. Their proximity, unless they happen to be married, should not be tolerated.

Lady Gough

The Mediterranean? Not any more, dear. It's the Elsan of Europe.

Alan Bennett

I'm glad to hear you smoke. A man should always have an occupation of some kind. There are far too many idle men in London as it is.

Oscar Wilde

You can get much further with a kind word and a gun than you can with a kind word alone.

Al Capone

I'd hate to drown. You look so awful afterwards.

Alan Ayckbourn

American women expect to find in their husbands a perfection that English women only hope to find in their butlers.

Somerset Maugham

We were so poor we didn't even have a lavatory brush. We used to tie my pet hedgehog to a stick and tell him to hold his breath.

Roy Brown

Sexual fidelity is not necessary to a well-conducted marriage. Your eldest son should certainly be your own, but beyond this it is excessively vulgar to enquire too closely into the paternity of your children.

Simon Raven

My brother has an unusual job – he finds things before other people lose them.

Frank Carson

I don't mind your smoking, if you don't mind my being sick all over you.

Thomas Beecham

When women kiss, it always reminds me of prize-fighters shaking hands.

H.L. Mencken

Kensington Gardens has been annexed as a middle-class rendezvous, and good society no longer goes there except to drown itself.

Princess Lieven

It is a fact that not once in my life have I gone out for a walk. I have been taken out for walks; but that is another matter.

Max Beerbohm

Anybody who has to ask what is the upkeep of a yacht cannot afford one.

J.P. Morgan

Why should we tolerate the system where a man with an amputated leg must get a medical certificate to state that the leg had not regrown each time he wants his allowances renewed?

Franklin Bicknell

Hypocrisy is the Vaseline of social intercourse.

J.R. Newman

I attribute my long and healthy life to the fact that I never touched a cigarette, a drink, or a girl until I was ten years old.

George Moore

To avoid lunatics on buses, sit in the middle of the bus. The friendly lunatics sit as close to the driver as they can, and the unfriendly ones sit as far away as they can.

Keith Allan Hunter

If you wait long enough beside the river you will see the bodies of your enemies float by.

Ying Chu

The true test is not whether a man behaves like a gentleman, but whether he misbehaves like one.

Sydney Tremayne

To every human problem there is a neat and easy solution – and it's wrong.

H.L. Mencken

A cigarette is the perfect type of a perfect pleasure. It is exquisite and leaves one quite unsatisfied. What more can one want?

Oscar Wilde

I wish I loved the human race;
I wish I loved its silly face;
I wish I liked the way it walks;
I wish I liked the way it talks;
And when I'm introduced to one
I wish I thought, What jolly fun.

Walter Raleigh

Blessed is he who expects no gratitude, for he shall not be disappointed.

W.C. Bennett

I was always unlawful; I broke the law when I was born because my parents weren't married.

George Bernard Shaw

Twenty-two acknowledged concubines and a library of sixty-two thousand volumes, attested the variety of the inclinations of the Emperor Gordian, and from the productions which he left behind him, it appears that the former as well as the latter were designed for use rather than ostentation.

Edward Gibbon

He was the sort of man who would throw a drowning man both ends of a rope.

Arthur Baer

You can measure the social caste of a person by the distance between the husband's and wife's apartments.

King Alfonso XIII

Every luxury was lavished on you – atheism, breastfeeding, circumcision.

Joe Orton

I think that black people should be given a fair crack of the whip.

Margaret Thatcher

Arson is not really a crime. There are many buildings that deserve to be burned down.

H. G. Wells

Always choose the oldest customs' official. No chance of promotion.

Somerset Maugham

Capital punishment is our society's recognition of the sanctity of human life.

Orrin Hatch

I much prefer travelling in non-British ships. There's none of that nonsense about women and children first.

Somerset Maugham

This is a free country. Folks have the right to send me letters, and I have the right not to open them.

William Faulkner

For parlour use the vague generality is a life-saver.

George Ade

To succeed in life it is not enough to be stupid. One must be well mannered as well.

Bonar Thompson

Mr Frick is the only man I know whom Dale Carnegie would have hit in the mouth.

Bill Veech

It was such a lovely day I thought it was a pity to get up.

Somerset Maugham

Yea, though I should walk through the valley of the shadow of death, I shall fear no evil, because I am the meanest son-of-a-bitch in the valley.

Gene M. Nordby

The great thing about suicide is that it's not one of those things you have to do now or lose your chance. You can always do it later.

Harvey Fierstein

Start off every day with a smile and get it over with.

W.C. Fields

Thirty-five is a very attractive age. London society is full of women who have of their own free choice remained thirty-five for years.

Oscar Wilde

You really have to get to know Dewey to dislike him.

Robert A. Taft

I should like one of these days to be so well known, so popular, so celebrated, so famous, that it would permit me to break wind in society and society would think it a most natural thing.

Honoré de Balzac

The members of the Aesthetic Movement between the wars spent on sodomy what they got by sponging.

George Orwell

I like long walks, especially when they are taken by people who annoy me.

Noel Coward

Half the world does not know how the other half lives, but is trying to find out.

Edgar W. Howe

I am in no need of your God damned sympathy. I ask only to be entertained by some of your grosser reminiscences.
Alexander Woollcott

Don't misunderstand me – my dislike for her is purely platonic.
Herbert Beerbohm Tree

At superior nudist camps, a nice class distinction was made; the butlers and maids who brought along the refreshments were forced to admit their lower social standing by wearing loincloths and aprons respectively.
Robert Graves

Never support two weaknesses at a time. It's your combination sinners – your lecherous liars and your miserly drunkards – who dishonour the vices and bring them into bad repute.
Thornton Wilder

When I want a peerage, I shall buy one like an honest man.
Lord Northcliffe

I have always regarded the telling of funny stories as the last refuge of the witless, the supreme consolation of dirty minded commercial travellers, wrenched from their homes and wireless sets.
Nathaniel Gubbins

The man who has cured himself of B.O. and halitosis, has learned French to surprise the waiter, and the saxophone to amuse the company, may find that people still avoid him because they do not like him.
Heywood Broun

The lie is the basic building block of good manners.
Quentin Crisp

No one really listens to anyone else, and if you try it for a while you will see why.

Mignon McLaughlin

To qualify as a member of the Women's Royal Voluntary Service you need to be able to wear a cardigan and jumper and a rope of pearls and to have had a hysterectomy.

Stella Reading

A bore is a man who when you ask him how he is, tells you.

B.L. Taylor

For seventeen years, George the Fifth did nothing at all but kill animals and stick in stamps.

Harold Nicolson

Because of the war shortages, there will be no napkins at dinner tonight. Instead, from time to time a woolly dog will pass among you.

Oscar Levant

The best indicator of a man's honesty isn't his income tax return. It's the zero adjustment on his bathroom scales.

Arthur C. Clarke

Beware of the conversationalist who adds 'in conclusion'. He is merely starting afresh.

Robert Morley

When I found a gibbet in an unexplored part of Africa, the sight of it gave me infinite pleasure, as it proved I was in a civilised society.

Mungo Park

If you think before you speak, the other fellow gets his joke in first.

Edgar W. Howe

Social Behaviour and Manners

'I believe I take precedence,' he said coldly; 'you are merely the club bore: I am the club liar.'

H.H. Munro

I loathe people who keep dogs. They are cowards who haven't the guts to bite people themselves.

August Strindberg

A healthy male adult bore consumes each year one and a half times his own weight in other people's patience.

John Updike

When the war broke out she took down the signed photograph of the Kaiser and, with some solemnity, hung it in the menservants' lavatory; it was her one combative action.

Evelyn Waugh

An interpreter is one who enables two persons of different languages to understand each other by repeating to each what it would have been to the interpreter's advantage for the other to have said.

Ambrose Bierce

It was said of Sarah, Duchess of Marlborough, that she never put dots over her i's, to save ink.

Horace Walpole

It's going to be fun to watch and see how long the meek can keep the earth after they inherit it.

Kin Hubbard

I like to visit my friends from time to time just to look over my library.

William Hazlitt

I see that the President of Rumania's mother is dead – there's always trouble for somebody.

Alan Bennett

I didn't have 3,000 pairs of shoes. I had only 1,060 pairs.

Imelda Marcos

If you desire to drain to the dregs the fullest cup of scorn and hatred that a fellow human being can pour out for you, let a young mother hear you call her baby 'it'.

Jerome K. Jerome

Sport

Football is all very well. A good game for rough girls, but not for delicate boys.

Oscar Wilde

Much as bookmakers are opposed to law-breaking they are not bigoted about it.

Damon Runyon

When Nicklaus plays well he wins; when he plays badly he comes second. When he plays terribly he's third.

Johnny Miller

If there is a thunderstorm on a golf course, walk down the middle of the fairway holding a one-iron over your head. Even God can't hit a one-iron.

Lee Trevino

He hit me among my face.

Henny Youngman

If the people don't want to come out to the ball park, nobody's gonna stop 'em.

Yogi Berra

There are fools, damn fools, and jockeys who remount in a steeplechase.

John Oaksey

This city has two great football teams – Liverpool and Liverpool reserves.

Bill Shankly

I've seen better swings than Bob Hope's in a condemned playground.

Arnold Palmer

Of course I have played outdoor games. I once played dominoes in an open air cafe in Paris.

Oscar Wilde

Never play cards with a man named Doc.

Nelson Algren

Some people think football is a matter of life and death. I don't like that attitude. I can assure them it is much more serious than that.

Bill Shankly

Women playing cricket should treat it as a matter between consenting females in private.

Michael Parkinson

Go jogging? What, and get hit by a meteor?

Robert Benchley

My grandfather couldn't prescribe a pill to make a greyhound run faster, but he could produce one to make the other five go slower.

Benny Green

When I got into the boxing ring women used to scream with delight because usually I'd left my shorts in the locker.

Roy Brown

That's what I call an airport shot. You hit one of those, you miss the cut and you're heading off for the airport.

Lee Trevino

The hardest thing about boxing is picking up your teeth with a boxing glove on.

Kin Hubbard

Anybody can win, unless there happens to be a second entry.
George Ade

The only exercise I ever get is taking the cuff-links out of one shirt and putting them in another.
Ring Lardner

Trust everybody – but cut the cards.
Finley Peter Dunne

You don't know what pressure is in golf until you play for five bucks with only two in your pocket.
Lee Trevino

Wales didn't even have enough imagination to thump someone in the line-out when the ref wasn't looking.
J.P.R. Williams

It is frequently asserted in bookmaking circles that my mother and father met only once and then for a very brief period.
Lord Wigg

Although he is a bad fielder, he is also a very poor hitter.
Ring Lardner

I have hunted deer on occasions, but they were not aware of it.
Felix Gear

The rules of soccer are basically simple – if it moves, kick it; if it doesn't move, kick it until it does.
Phil Woosnam

I failed to make the chess team because of my height.
Woody Allen

Losing the Super Bowl is worse than death. With death you don't have to get up next morning.

George Allen

A fishing rod is a stick with a worm at one end and a fool at the other.

Samuel Johnson

A proper definition of an amateur sportsman today is one who accepts cash, not cheques.

Jack Kelly

Life is just an elaborate metaphor for cricket.

Marvin Cohen

I cannot see who is leading in the Boat Race, but it's either Oxford or Cambridge.

John Snagge

I went to a fight the other night and a hockey game broke out.

Rodney Dangerfield

The race is not always to the swift, nor the battle to the strong – but that's the way to bet.

Damon Runyon

I want to thank all the people who made this meeting necessary.

Yogi Berra

Never play tennis for money against a grey-haired player.

Tom Robinson

When I was a coach at Rochester they called me in and said 'We're making a change in your department.' I was the only guy in my department.

Don Cherry

Sport

Footballers are miry gladiators whose sole purpose in life is to position a surrogate human head between two poles.

Elizabeth Hogg

Winning isn't everything – it's the only thing.

Vince Lombardi

There is plenty of time to win this game, and to trash the Spaniards too – my bowels cannot wait.

Francis Drake

My horse was in the lead, coming down the home stretch, but the caddie fell off.

Samuel Goldwyn

Herbert Strudwick used to recommend to wicket-keepers 'Rinse your hands in the chamber pot every day. The urine hardens them wonderfully.'

David Lemmon

Skiing combines outdoor fun with knocking down trees with your face.

Dave Barry

You can observe a lot just by watching.

Yogi Berra

If you want a track team to win the high jump, you find one person who can jump seven feet, not seven people who can each jump one foot.

Frederick E. Terman

I'd give my right arm to get back into the England team.

Peter Shilton

Remember, postcards only, please. The winner will be the first one opened.

Brian Moore

A computer once beat me at chess, but it was no match for me at kick boxing.

Emo Philips

The British Board of Censors will not pass any seduction scene unless the seducer has one foot on the floor. Apparently sex in England is something like snooker.

Fred Allen

What a terrible round. I only hit two good balls all day and that was when I stepped on a rake in a bunker.

Lee Trevino

Pro basketball coaching is when you wake up in the morning and wish your parents had never met.

Bill Fitch

Remember, it doesn't matter whether you win or lose; what matters is whether I win or lose.

Darrin Weinberg

I'm going to win so much money this year that my caddie will make the top twenty money-winners list.

Lee Trevino

I promised I would take Rotherham out of the second division. I did – into the third division.

Tommy Docherty

I'd like to borrow Muhammad Ali's body for just forty-eight hours. There are three guys I'd like to beat up and four women I'd like to make love to.

Jim Murray

You can have sex either before cricket or after cricket – the fundamental fact is that cricket must be there at the centre of things.

Harold Pinter

If at first you don't succeed – so much for skydiving.

Henny Youngman

I resigned as coach because of illness and fatigue. The fans were sick and tired of me.

John Ralston

Football combines the worst features of American life – frantic violence punctuated by committee meetings.

George Will

Grouse shooting begins on August 12th. A grouse shot before that date tends to be very annoyed.

Michael Shea

We should be thankful to lynch mobs. I've got a brother who can run a half mile faster than any white boy in the world.

Dick Gregory

A sportsman is a man who, every now and then, simply has to get out and kill something.

Stephen Leacock

Look laddie, if you're in the penalty area and aren't quite sure what to do with the ball, just stick it in the net and we'll discuss all your options afterwards.

Bill Shankly

The athletic facilities situation is a mess. Girls still haven't figured out how to use the urinals.

John Roberts

Of course there should be women basketball referees.
Incompetence should not be confined to one sex.

Bill Russell

When Nastase is winning, he's objectionable. When he's
losing, he's highly objectionable.

Adrian Clark

I'll fine any of my players who wins the Lady Byng Trophy
for ice hockey gentlemanly conduct.

Punch Imlach

There are few tactical rules for mixed doubles. One is to hit
the girl whenever possible.

Bill Tilden

Anyone who burns a cross on my lawn, he won't burn
anything ever again if I catch him.

Sonny Liston

My golfing partner couldn't hit a tiled floor with a bellyful
of puke.

David Feherty

Give me my golf clubs, fresh air and a beautiful partner, and
you can keep my golf clubs and the fresh air.

Jack Benny

Monica Seles – I'd hate to be next door to her on her
wedding night.

Peter Ustinov

I've seen George Foreman shadow boxing and the shadow
won.

Muhammad Ali

263

In the World Darts Championships in 1982, Jocky Wilson
missed when attempting to shake hands with an opponent.
Craig Brown

Golf is an ineffectual attempt to direct an uncontrollable
sphere into an inaccessible hole with instruments ill-adapted
to the purpose.

Winston Churchill

W.G. Grace had one of the dirtiest necks I ever kept wicket
behind.

George Cobham

I am to cricket what Dame Sybil Thorndyke is to nonferrous
welding.

Frank Muir

Never catch a loose horse. You could end up all day holding
the f•••••• thing.

Lester Piggott

Golf is so popular simply because it is the best game in the
world at which to be bad.

A.A. Milne

She leads away from aces and neglects to keep my jump bids
alive. But she is still my mother.

Heywood Broun

Professional wrestling's most mystifying hold is on its
audience.

Luke Neely

Moving from Wales to Italy is like going to a different
country.

Ian Rush

I love Liverpool so much that if I caught one of their players in bed with my missus I'd tiptoe downstairs and make him a cup of tea.

A. Koppite

If I had to choose between sex and snooker, I'd choose snooker.

Steve Davis

I have a bad swing, a bad stance and a bad grip, but my bank manager loves me.

Lee Trevino

Perhaps if I dyed my hair peroxide blond and called myself the great white tadpole, that would help.

Ian Woosnam

One should always play fairly when one has the winning cards.

Oscar Wilde

I object to hare coursing on the grounds that real men should tear the live hares apart with their own teeth. Why should the dogs have all the fun?

Ernest Hemingway

The man who caught that fish is a liar.

George Robey

I don't like money, actually, but I find it quiets my nerves.

Joe Louis

The amateur rugby union player has an inalienable right to play like a pillock.

Dick Greenwood

The trouble with referees is that they just don't care which side wins.

Tom Canterbury

I am not my brother's wicketkeeper.

Clyde Packer

People started calling me 'Fiery' because 'Fiery' rhymes with 'Fred' just like 'Typhoon' rhymes with 'Tyson'.

Fred Trueman

With good practice at high level diving you can avoid killing yourself.

Elizabeth MacKay

If me and King Kong went into an alley, only one of us would come out. And it wouldn't be the monkey.

Lyle Alzado

Al Davis is a very smart man. He's probably the only one who knows the serial number of the Unknown Soldier.

Sam Rutigliano

I've never seen such skinny legs on a football player before. I wonder if he ever caught the rustler who stole his calves?

Steve Jordan

In running you have to be suspicious when you line up against girls with moustaches.

Maree Holland

Anyone who doesn't watch rugby league is not a real person. He's a cow's hoof, an ethnic, senile or comes from Melbourne.

John Singleton

Modern rugby players like to get their retaliation in first.

Kim Fletcher

If a lot of people gripped a knife and fork like they do a golf club, they'd starve to death.

Sam Snead

Boxing is a lot of white men watching two black men beat each other up.

Muhammad Ali

Golf is like an eighteen-year-old girl with big boobs. You know it's wrong but you can't keep away from her.

Val Doonican

Rugby is a ruffian's game played by gentlemen; soccer is a gentlemen's game played by ruffians; and Gaelic football is a ruffian's game played by ruffians.

Patrick Murray

The first time I saw Walter Payton in the locker room, I thought, God must have taken a hammer and said to Himself, 'I'm going to make me a half-back'.

Fred O'Connor

Skiing? Why should I break my leg at forty degrees below zero when I can fall downstairs at home?

Corey Ford

The Gullikson twins, Tim and Tom, are both from Wisconsin.

Dan Maskell

I saw Joe Di Maggio last night and he wasn't wearing his baseball suit. This struck me as rather foolish. Suppose a ball game broke out in the middle of the night? By the time he got into his suit the game would be over.

Groucho Marx

It took me seventeen years to get three thousand hits in baseball. I did it in one afternoon on the golf course.

Henry Aaron

What they say about footballers being ignorant is rubbish. I spoke to a couple yesterday and they were quite intelligent.

Raquel Welch

Fate was kind to him, dealing him a hand of five aces.

Harry Wilson

Being a manager is simple. All you have to do is to keep the five players who hate your guts away from the five who are undecided.

Casey Stengel

I see two fellows in the ring; I hit the one that isn't there and the one that is there hits me.

Billy Softly

I am donating a shilling to W.G. Grace's testimonial not in support of cricket, but as an earnest protest against golf.

Max Beerbohm

Last time we got a penalty away from home, Christ was still a carpenter.

Lennie Lawrence

A bookie is just a pickpocket who lets you use your own hands.

Henry Morgan

Yes we've had bad times at Anfield; one year we came second.

Bob Paisley

I refuse to play golf with Errol Flynn. If I want to play with a prick, I'll play with my own.

W.C. Fields

Baseball is very big with my people. It's the only time we can get to shake a bat at a white man without starting a riot.

Dick Gregory

If you ever get belted and see three fighters through a haze, go after the one in the middle. That's what ruined me – I went after the two guys on the end.

Max Baer

If Stan Bowles could pass a betting shop like he can pass a football, he'd have no worries at all.

Ernie Tagg

I shall continue to give relegated Luton my full support – in fact I'm wearing it at this very moment.

Eric Morecambe

Now that I have won the Olympic heavyweight weight-lifting gold medal, maybe my wife will show more respect.

Vasily Alexeyev

I have seen players, famous internationals, in an airport lounge all get up and follow one bloke to the toilet. Six of them maybe, all standing there not wanting a piss themselves, but following the bloke who does.

Geoff Hurst

My definition of a foreigner is someone who doesn't understand cricket.

Anthony Couch

Gary Lineker is the Queen Mother of football.

James Christopher

I never play cricket. It requires one to assume such indecent postures.

Oscar Wilde

The only reason I would take up jogging is so I could hear heavy breathing again.

Erma Bombeck

 **Sport**

They can get a man on the moon but they cannot get a man on Martina Navratilova.

Roy Brown

Theatre and Criticism

I have knocked everything in this play except the chorus
girls' knees, and there God anticipated me.

Percy Hammond

If laughter is contagious, my son has found the cure.

Les Dawson's mother

You wouldn't get away with that if my script writer was
here.

Bob Hope

I saw the play under adverse conditions – the curtain was up.

Robert Benchley

If there are any of you at the back who do not hear me, there
is no use raising your hands because I am also near-sighted.

W.H. Auden

Chevy Chase couldn't ad-lib a fart after a baked bean dinner.

Johnny Carson

A first night audience consists of the unburied dead.

Orson Bean

Critics are like eunuchs in a harem; they know exactly how
it should be done – they see it being done every night, but
they can't do it themselves.

Brendan Behan

Waiting For Godot is a play in which nothing happens, twice.

Vivian Mercier

The impact of the play was like the banging together of two
damp dish-cloths.

Brendan Behan

Two things in the play should have been cut. The second act and that youngster's throat.

Noel Coward

My agent gets ten per cent of everything I get, except the blinding headaches.

Fred Allen

The play was a great success, but the audience was a disaster.

Oscar Wilde

No one can have a higher opinion of him than I have – and I think he is a dirty little beast.

W.S. Gilbert

There is absolutely nothing wrong with Oscar Levant that a miracle cannot fix.

Alexander Woollcott

The central problem in *Hamlet* is whether the critics are mad or only pretending to be mad.

Oscar Wilde

He played the King as if he was afraid that at any moment someone would play the ace.

Eugene Field

Robert Mitchum does not so much act as point his suit at people.

Russell Davies

Go on writing plays my boy. One of these days a London producer will go into his office and say to his secretary, 'Is there a play from Shaw this morning?' and when she says 'No,' he will say, 'Well, then we'll have to start on the rubbish.' And that's your chance my boy.

George Bernard Shaw

Asking a writer what he thinks about critics is like asking a lamp-post what it thinks about dogs.

John Osborne

I like work; it fascinates me. I can sit and look at it for hours.

Jerome K. Jerome

Comedy, like sodomy, is an unnatural act.

Marty Feldman

There is less in this play than meets the eye.

Tallulah Bankhead

What is *Uncle Vanya* about? I would say it is about as much as I can take.

Roger Garland

I can take any amount of criticism, so long as it is unqualified praise.

Noel Coward

What is the play about? It's about to make me a great deal of money.

Tom Stoppard

I go to the theatre to be entertained. I don't want to see rape, sodomy, incest and drug addiction. I can get all of that at home.

Peter Cook

Liza Minelli comes out looking like a giant rodent en route to a costume ball.

Stanley Kauffmann

Critics are pygmies with poison darts who live in the valley of the sleeping giants.

Dagobert D. Runes

My reputation grows with every failure.

George Bernard Shaw

One of the first and most important things for a critic to learn is how to sleep undetected at the theatre.

William Archer

They are going to dig up Shakespeare and dig up Bacon; they are going to get Beerbohm Tree to recite *Hamlet* to them, and the one who turns in his coffin will be the author of the play.

W.S. Gilbert

The secret of my great talent as an actor is that I speak in a loud clear voice and try not to bump into the furniture.

Alfred Lunt

An actress is someone with no ability who sits around waiting to go on alimony.

Jackie Stallone

One of my chief regrets during my years in the theatre is that I couldn't sit in the audience and watch myself.

John Barrymore

Actresses are another kettle of bitch.

Gilbert Harding

Scratch an actor – and you'll find an actress.

Dorothy Parker

In England nobody goes to the theatre unless he or she has bronchitis.

James Agate

A fan club is a group of people who tell an actor that he is not alone in the way he feels about himself.

Jack Carson

Some of the greatest love affairs I have known involved one
actor, unassisted.

Wilson Mizner

Sarah Bernhardt is a great actress from the waist down.

Margaret Kendal

The scenery was beautiful – but the actors got in front of it.

Alexander Woollcott

O Calcutta is the sort of show that gives pornography a bad
name.

Clive Barnes

My dear sir, I have read your play. Oh, my dear sir.

Herbert Beerbohm Tree

Depending upon shock tactics is easy, whereas writing a
good play is difficult. Pubic hair is no substitute for wit.

J.B. Priestley

Richard Burton as Caliban looked like a miner with a tail
coming up from a coal face.

James Agate

The plot of *Who Killed Agatha Christie* has as many holes as a
sieve and is far less entertaining.

Bernard Levin

If she were cast as Lady Godiva, the horse would steal the
show.

Patrick Murray

Sarah Brightman couldn't act scared on the New York
subway at four o'clock in the morning.

Joel Segal

Only one joke of *Rose Marie* was applauded: 'We are all going into the fitting room to have a fit.' This kind of brilliance was not sustained.

Clive Barnes

In Tyrone Guthrie's production of *Hamlet*, Mr Frederick Bennett's first gravedigger is the one gloomy spot in the entire production.

James Agate

Richard Briers last night played Hamlet like a demented typewriter.

W.A. Darlington

Stephen Fry has all the wit of an unflushed toilet.

Bernard Manning

Peter O'Toole delivers every line with a monotonous tenor bark as if addressing an audience of deaf Eskimos.

Michael Billington

The play left a taste of lukewarm parsnip juice.

Alexander Woollcott

A star is anyone who has shaken hands with Lew Grade, and a superstar is someone who has refused to shake hands with Lew Grade.

Harry Secombe

Elizabeth Taylor – just how garish her commonplace accent, her squeakily shrill voice, and the childish petulance with which she delivers her lines are, my pen is neither scratchy nor leaky enough to convey.

John Simon

Edith Sitwell is like a high altar on the move.

Elizabeth Bowen

He wanted to be an actor. He had all the qualifications, including no money and a total lack of responsibility.

Hedda Hopper

I don't believe in dying. It's been done. I'm working on a new exit. Besides, I can't die now – I'm booked.

George Burns

A plagiarist is a writer of plays.

Oscar Wilde

I got all the schooling an actress needs – I learned to write enough to sign contracts.

Hermione Gingold

You can tell how bad a musical is by the number of times the chorus yells 'hooray'.

John Crosby

Miscellaneous

The realisation that one is to be hanged in the morning concentrates the mind wonderfully.

Samuel Johnson

There is only one way to find out if a man is honest – ask him. If he says 'yes' he's not honest.

Groucho Marx

Never kick a fresh turd on a hot day.

Harry S. Truman

The kilt is an unrivalled garment for fornication and diarrhoea.

John Masters

A filing cabinet is a place where you can lose things systematically.

T.H. Thompson

The snowdrop is more powerful than the Panzer.

Beverley Nichols

Princess Anne is such an active lass. So outdoorsy. She loves nature in spite of what nature did to her.

Bette Midler

It is always the best policy to tell the truth, unless of course you happen to be an exceptionally good liar.

Jerome K. Jerome

The reports of my death have been greatly exaggerated.

Mark Twain

One morning I shot an elephant in my pyjamas. How he got in my pyjamas I'll never know.

Groucho Marx

I know the answer! The answer lies within the heart of mankind! The answer is twelve? I must be in the wrong book.

Charles Schultz

Summer has set in with its usual severity.

S. T. Coleridge

See the happy moron, he doesn't give a damn. I wish I were a moron: my God, perhaps I am.

R. Fairchild

Rumpers was a little man. He made no secret of his height.

Alan Bennett

Just how big a coward am I? Well I was on the Olympic team.

Bob Hope

I have too much respect for the truth to drag it out on every trifling occasion.

Mark Twain

Always look out for number one and be careful not to step in number two.

Rodney Dangerfield

Too intense contemplation of his own genius had begun to undermine his health.

Max Beerbohm

I used to sell furniture for a living. The trouble was, it was my own.

Les Dawson

I'm not afraid of heights but I'm afraid of widths.

Steven Wright

There is nothing safer than flying – it's crashing that is dangerous.

Theo Cowan

One, two, three
Buckle my shoe.

Robert Benchley

A pedestrian is anyone who is knocked down by a motor car.

J.B. Morton

I never forget a face, but in your case I'm willing to make an exception.

Groucho Marx

One should try everything once, except incest and folk-dancing.

Arnold Bax

The trouble with this country is that there are too many people going about saying 'The trouble with this country is ...'

Sinclair Lewis

If dirt was trumps, what a hand you would hold!

Charles Lamb

I resigned from the army after two weeks service in the field, explaining I was 'incapacitated by fatigue' through persistent retreating.

Mark Twain

A committee is a cul-de-sac into which ideas are lured and then quietly strangled.

John A. Lincoln

On a Polar expedition begin with a clear idea which Pole you are aiming at, and try to start facing the right way. Choose your companions carefully – you may have to eat them.

W.C. Sellar

Go, and never darken my towels again.

Groucho Marx

The toilet paper was composed of quartered sheets of typing paper, with holes in one corner. These were covered in messages, many of them marked 'Secret' and some of them marked 'Top Secret'.

Peter Ustinov

The human race, to which so many of my readers belong ...

G.K. Chesterton

The dog was licking its private parts with the gusto of an alderman drinking soup.

Graham Greene

Such time as he can spare from the adornment of his person he devotes to the neglect of his duties.

Samuel Johnson

Always remember the poor – it costs nothing.

Josh Billings

'I'm very brave generally,' he went on in a low voice: 'only today I happen to have a headache.'

Lewis Carroll

No problem is insoluble, given a big enough plastic bag.

Tom Stoppard

Death is psychosomatic.

Charles Manson

I had a terrific idea this morning but I didn't like it.
Samuel Goldwyn

Self-decapitation is an extremely difficult, not to say dangerous thing to attempt.
W.S. Gilbert

I don't know what effect these men will have upon the enemy, but, by God, they terrify me.
Duke of Wellington

The most hazardous part of our expedition to Africa was crossing Piccadilly Circus.
Joseph Thomson

I admire Cecil Rhodes, I frankly confess it; and when the time comes I shall buy a piece of the rope for a keepsake.
Mark Twain

The biggest fool in the world hasn't been born yet.
Josh Billings

Guy Burgess had the look of an inquisitive rodent emerging into daylight from a drain.
Harold Nicolson

A large body of men have expressed their willingness to serve in the Army against Napoleon subject to the condition that they should not be sent overseas – except I presume in case of invasion.
William Pitt

What happens to the holes when the Swiss cheese is eaten?
Bertolt Brecht

The lion and the calf shall lie down together but the calf won't get much sleep.

Woody Allen

Another victory like that and we are done for.

Pyrrhus

I have bad reflexes. I was once run over by a car being pushed by two guys.

Woody Allen

I can believe anything as long as it is incredible.

Oscar Wilde

The man who would stoop so low as to write an anonymous letter, the least he might do is to sign his name to it.

Boyle Roach

A man cannot be in two places at the same time unless he is a bird.

Boyle Roach

'I will only shake my finger at him,' he said, and placed it on the trigger.

Stanislaw J. Lec

No man is an island but some of us are pretty long peninsulas.

Ashleigh Brilliant

Underground we have coal for 600 years. Above it we have Mr Shinwell. Reversal of these positions would solve our present troubles.

R.A. Whitsun

According to the Law of the West, a Colt 45 beats four aces.

Bill Jones

As I hurtled through space, one thought kept crossing my mind – every part of this capsule was supplied by the lowest bidder.

John Glynn

Kindly inform troops immediately that all communications have broken down.

Ashleigh Brilliant

There are two classes of people in the world – those who divide people into two classes and those who don't.

Robert Benchley

If you think the problem is bad now, just wait until we've solved it.

Arthur Kasspe

Dogs are sons of bitches.

W.C. Fields

I was brought up to respect my elders so now I don't have to respect anybody.

George Burns

I haven't killed anyone all day – help me keep it that way.

Clint Eastwood

What smells so? Has somebody been burning a rag or is there a dead mule in the back yard? No, the man is smoking a five-cent cigar.

Eugene Field

You can have an affection for a murderer or a sodomite, but you cannot have an affection for a man whose breath stinks.

George Orwell

In the space age, man will be able to go around the world in two hours – one hour for flying and the other to get to the airport.

Neil M. McElroy

Don't stand around doing nothing – people will think you're just a workman.

Spike Milligan

Cleopatra had the body of a roll-top desk and the mind of a duck.

Rowan Atkinson

If everyone minded their own business, the world would go round a great deal faster than it does.

Lewis Carroll

It may be December outside, ladies, but under your armpits, it is always August.

John Snagge

To write a diary every day is like returning to one's own vomit.

Enoch Powell

A Coarse Sailor is one who in a crisis forgets nautical language and shouts, 'For God's sake turn left.'

Michael Green

Many a man who can't direct you to a corner drugstore will get a respectful hearing when age has further impaired his mind.

Finley Peter Dunne

It is not enough to succeed – others must fail.

Gore Vidal

Yesterday was the first day of the rest of your life and you messed it up again.

Patrick Murray

I talk to myself a lot, but it bothers some people because I use a megaphone.

Steven Wright

The private papers that Herbert Morrison left behind were so dull and banal that they would provide illumination only if they were burned.

Greg Knight

Nero renamed the month of April after himself, calling it Neroneus, but the idea never caught on because April is not Neroneus and there is no use pretending that it is.

Will Cuppy

One day I sat thinking, almost in despair; a hand fell on my shoulder and a voice said reassuringly, 'Cheer up, things could be worse.' So I cheered up, and sure enough, things got worse.

James Hagerty

I believe in opening my mail once a month – whether it needs it or not.

Bob Considine

If it weren't for bad luck I wouldn't have any luck at all.

Dick Gregory

My car had only one previous owner – Coco the clown.

Lenny Windsor

If I had known I was going to live so long I would have taken better care of myself.

Leon Eldred

I can only hope that when the enemy reads the list of my officers' names he trembles as I do.

Duke of Wellington

Some people are always late, like the late King George V.

Spike Milligan

The object of war is not to die for your country but to make the other bastard die for his.

George Patton

I'd like to be a procrastinator, but I never seem to get around to it.

Chris Dundee

Never mistake motion for action.

Ernest Hemingway

Hard work never killed anybody, but why take a chance on being the first?

Edgar Bergen

Take the diplomacy out of war and the thing would fall flat in a week.

Will Rogers

QANTAS is a condom on the penis of progress.

Ian Tuxworth

I'm about as useful as a one-legged man at an arse-kicking contest.

Dave Dutton

Neil Armstrong was the first man to walk on the moon. I'm the first man to piss his pants on the moon.

Buzz Aldrin

They are not really fixing the streets. They are just moving the holes around so the motorists cannot memorise them.

Herb Shriner

According to my contract, I get fifty dollars from the management every time someone calls me 'nigger'. Please do it again. Let's have the whole audience stand up and do it in unison! I'll retire tomorrow.

Dick Gregory

I'm gonna be so tough as mayor I'm gonna make Attila the Hun look like a faggot.

Frank Rizzo

Every place I look at I work out the cubic feet and I say it will make a good warehouse or it won't. Can't help myself. One of the best warehouses I ever did see was the Vatican in Rome.

Arnold Wesker

Mother Hubbard was old, alone, and a widow – a friendless, old, solitary widow. Yet, did she despair? Did she sit down and weep or read a novel, or wring her hands? No! She went to the cupboard.

Lord Desart

I have a lot of fun in the summer time. People come up, slap me on the back and I say 'Watch it! My sunburn.' You'd be surprised how many apologies I get.

Dick Gregory

They couldn't hit an elephant at this dist ...

General Sedgwick

Drawing on my fine command of language, I said nothing.

Robert Benchley

It always looks darkest just before it gets totally black.

Charlie Brown

If you're there before it's over, you're on time.

James J. Walker

Mick Jagger has big lips. I once saw him suck an egg out of a chicken.

Joan Rivers

The Royal Navy – rum, sodomy, and the lash.

Winston Churchill

Would you like to find out what it's like to be a member of a minority group? Try putting in an honest day's work occasionally.

Kelly Fordyce

Epitaph for a dead waiter – God finally caught his eye.

George S. Kaufman

A lot of people have been asking why there are no Negro astronauts. Well, I've got a surprise for you. One of those seven boys is. He's just looked white since they told him what he volunteered for.

Dick Gregory

Never play leapfrog with a unicorn.

Michael Shea

William F. Buckley looks and sounds not unlike Hitler – but without the charm.

Gore Vidal

It's great to be with Bill Buckley, because you don't have to think. He takes a position and you automatically take the opposite one and you know you're right.

J.K. Galbraith

You had to stand in line to hate Harry Cohn.

Hedda Hopper

I have my standards. They may be low, but I have them.

Bette Midler

The trouble with doing nothing is that you can never take any time off.

Hoagy Carmichael

There is no limit to how complicated things can get, on account of one thing always leading to another.

E.B. White

If it's not one thing, it's two.

James Ledford

I have never killed a man, but I have read many obituaries with a lot of pleasure.

Clarence Darrow

No issue is so small that it can't be blown out of proportion.

Stuart Hughes

More than any time in history mankind faces a crossroads. One path leads to despair and utter hopelessness, the other to total destruction. Let us pray that we have the wisdom to choose correctly.

Woody Allen

I have a memory like an elephant. In fact elephants often consult me.

Noel Coward

I was going to buy a copy of *The Power of Positive Thinking* and then I thought 'What the hell good would that do?'

Ronald Shakes

Too bad that all the people who know how to run the country are busy driving taxicabs or cutting hair.

George Burns

He must have had a magnificent build before his stomach went in for a career of its own.

Margaret Halsley

I had to give up masochism – I was enjoying it too much.

Mel Calman

The pen is mightier than the sword – and considerably easier to write with.

Marty Feldman

E.W.B. Nicholson, Bodley's Librarian, spent three days at the London Docks, watching outgoing ships, after losing a book at the Bodley, which was afterwards discovered slightly out of place on the shelf.

Falconer Madan

A diplomat is a person who can tell you to go to hell in such a way that you actually look forward to the trip.

Caskie Stinnet

What was the war like? My dear fellow it was awful – the noise, and the people!

W.H. Auden

Miscellaneous

The first thing I do in the morning is to read the obituaries
in *The Times* and if I am not in them I get up.

Noel Coward

In the battle of wits, Frank Fay entered the skirmish almost
totally unarmed.

Milton Berle

I hate the poor and look forward eagerly to their
extermination.

George Bernard Shaw

Anything that man says you've got to take with a dose of
salts.

Samuel Goldwyn

Have you ever noticed that wrong numbers are never
engaged?

Steven Wright

Whenever I feel like exercise, I lie down until the feeling passes.
R.M. Hutchins

When I was young, I was told: 'You'll see, when you're fifty.' I
am fifty and I haven't seen a thing.

Eric Satie

I once had a rose named after me and I was very flattered.
But I was not pleased to read the description in the
catalogue: no good in a bed, but fine up against a wall.

Eleanor Roosevelt

Auntie did you feel no pain
Falling from that apple tree?
Would you do it, please again,
'Cos my friend here didn't see?

Harry Graham

Watch out when you're getting all you want: only hogs being fattened for the slaughter get all they want.

Joel Chandler Harris

There is no more agreeable spectacle than to observe an old friend fall from a roof-top.

Confucius

Saturday morning, although recurring at regular and well foreseen intervals, always seems to take Baker Street Station by surprise.

W.S. Gilbert

Never make excuses, never let them see you bleed, and never get separated from your baggage.

Wesley Price

They made me a present of Mornington Crescent – they threw it a brick at a time.

Albert Chevalier

I don't know what my dog's real name is but I call him 'Rover'.

Stafford Beer

A Jewish nymphomaniac is a woman who will make love with a man the same day she has her hair done.

Maureen Lipman

Middle age is when you are sitting at home on a Saturday night and the telephone rings and you hope it isn't for you.

Ogden Nash

The method preferred by most balding men for making themselves look silly is called the 'comb-over' which is when the man grows the hair on one side of his head very long and combs it across the bald area, creating an effect that looks from the top like an egg in the grasp of a large tropical spider.

Dave Barry

I got some new underwear the other day. Well, new to me.

Emo Philips

Who invented the brush they put next to the toilet? That thing hurts.

Andy Andrews

It's a small world, but I wouldn't like to have to paint it.

Steven Wright

If you've got them by the balls, their hearts and minds will follow.

John Wayne

The answer is in the plural and they bounce.

Edwin Lutyens

My neighbour asked if he could use my lawnmower and I told him of course he could so long as he didn't take it out of my garden.

Eric Morecambe

A collision is what happens when two motorists go after the same pedestrian.

Bob Newhart

I have so much to do that I am going to bed.

Robert Benchley

'Victorian Apartment' means that the bedrooms have only enough space for one tightly bound woman.

Wes Smith

Do you know how helpless you feel if you have a cupful of coffee in your hand and you start to sneeze?

Jean Kerr

You cannot have everything. I mean where would you put it?

Steven Wright

Index

Index

Index

Index

Index

Index

Index

Index

Index

Index